Unders
La..

They are playing a game. They are playing at not playing a game. If I show them I see they are, I shall break the rules and they will punish me. I must play their game, of not seeing I see the game.

RD Laing, *Knots.*

First published.. *1974*
Second impression.. *1974*
Third impression.. *1975*
Revised edition.. *1978*
Second impression revised edition.. *1980*
Second edition.. *1984*
Second impression second edition.. *1987*
Third edition.. *1988*

Drawings by Yolande Bull

Understanding Law

an introduction to Australia's legal system

Fourth edition

RICHARD CHISHOLM BA, LL B (Syd), BCL (Oxon)
Associate Professor of Law, University of New South Wales

GARTH NETTHEIM AM (Tufts USA), LL B (Syd)
Professor of Law, University of New South Wales

BUTTERWORTHS
Sydney — Adelaide — Brisbane — Canberra — Hobart
Melbourne — Perth
1992

The Hand and Star

Trademark of Butterworths Australia

This colophon, dating back to 1553, is almost as old as legal publishing itself.

Richard Tottel, a printer, opened a business at No 7 Fleet Street within London's Temple Bar and hung out his sign, choosing a hand, symbol of authority, holding the star of knowledge shedding light on the law.

In 1818 Henry Butterworth acquired the company which displayed the 'Hand and Starre'. This unique symbol became the official trademark in 1895 and continues to be the insignia of Butterworths Australia.

AUSTRALIA	BUTTERWORTHS 271–273 Lane Cove Road, North Ryde 2113 Vanguard Insurance Building, 195 Victoria Square, Adelaide 5000 Commonwealth Bank Building, King George Square, Brisbane 4000 53–55 Northbourne Avenue, Canberra 2601 20 Runnymede Street, Battery Point 7004 160 William Street, Melbourne 3000 178 St Georges Terrace, Perth 6000
CANADA	BUTTERWORTHS CANADA LTD Toronto and Vancouver
IRELAND	BUTTERWORTH (IRELAND) LTD Dublin
MALAYSIA	MALAYAN LAW JOURNAL SDN BHD Kuala Lumpur
NEW ZEALAND	BUTTERWORTHS OF NEW ZEALAND LTD Wellington and Auckland
PUERTO RICO	BUTTERWORTH OF PUERTO RICO INC San Juan
SINGAPORE	BUTTERWORTHS ASIA Singapore
UNITED KINGDOM	BUTTERWORTH & CO (PUBLISHERS) LTD London and Edinburgh
USA	BUTTERWORTH LEGAL PUBLISHERS Austin, Texas; Clearwater, Florida; Orford, New Hampshire; St Paul, Minnesota; Salem, New Hampshire

National Library of Australia Cataloguing-in-Publication entry

Chisholm, Richard (Richard Colin), 1944– .
Understanding law: an introduction to Australia's legal system.

4th ed. Bibliography. Includes index.
ISBN 0 409 30486 7.

1. Law — Australia. 2. Justice, Administration of — Australia. I. Nettheim, Garth. II. Title.

347.94

Inquiries should be addressed to the publishers.
Typeset in Australia by Post Typesetters, Brisbane.
Printed in Australia by Star Printery Pty Ltd.

Contents

Acknowledgments

We are grateful to Simon Rice for comments on the draft of Chapter 11, and to a number of our colleagues who provided comments on some chapters of the second and third editions: Regina Graycar, Owen Jessep, David Neal and Paul Redmond. We also thank Sue Yeomans for preparing the index. According to the time-honoured tradition, we announce that any flaws in the final product are our responsibility, not theirs. Nevertheless, we secretly hope, dear reader, that in the unlikely event that you may find any error, infelicity of expression or bad joke, you will attribute it to one, or even all, of them.

Preface to the Fourth Edition

When we prepared our preface for the Third Edition, published in 1988, it was timely to focus on the Bicentennial celebrations and particularly to reflect on the legacies of two centuries of English-based law: firstly, in displacing and dispossessing Australia's Aboriginal peoples and their law, and secondly (and less adequately) in resolving outstanding issues. The 1991 Report of the *Royal Commission Into Aboriginal Deaths in Custody* shows that the need to resolve these issues is as urgent as ever, yet resolution remains elusive. At the time of writing, the Federal Government's 1988 commitment to negotiate a treaty (strongly opposed by the Opposition) has been superseded by a 1991 Act, passed with bipartisan support, to establish a *Council on Aboriginal Reconciliation* with a mandate to seek reconciliation and (possibly) to propose an instrument or instruments in time for the Centenary of Federation in 2001. And the High Court's landmark decision in *Mabo v Queensland* for the first time clearly acknowledged that indigenous land rights have, to some extent, survived the arrival of British law.

Those issues remain with us in 1991. But they also appear in the interesting context of a Federal Government seeking to project a more independent national image (particularly by moving away from former British associations) while also becoming more closely involved in international relationships. The latter development has a particular relevance to the Aboriginal issues: in October 1992, the General Assembly of the United Nations will inaugurate 1993 as the *International Year of the World's Indigenous Peoples*. And a United

Nations Working Group has set 1992 as the date for completion of the drafting of a Universal Declaration on the Rights of Indigenous Peoples.

Other international instruments, particularly in the field of human rights, become of increasing relevance to Australia, particularly since 25 December 1991 when Australia's ratification of the *First Optional Protocol to the International Covenant on Civil and Political Rights* took effect. This action provides the first (but presumably not the last) opportunity for Australians to communicate directly to an international agency (the Human Rights Committee) charging Australia with failing to comply with its international obligations under the Convention. That and other international human rights treaties such as the *Convention on the Rights of the Child*, which Australia ratified in 1990, provide for a system of international scrutiny of Australia's performance in a number of areas of human rights.

International developments, therefore, have become increasingly influential in the continuing development of Australian law. Perhaps this is true of all countries. Population increases, growing threats to the environment, and tensions associated with the huge gap between the affluent West and the famine and poverty in many Third World countries are increasingly being seen as problems that require international co-operation and, where law is relevant, international treaties as well as national laws.

The increasing impact of international affairs on Australia's "domestic" law provides an example of a theme that is stressed in this book, especially in this Fourth Edition. The theme is that Australian law does not stand alone. It has been shaped by historical factors, and it is constantly changing in response to external forces which exist at a local, national and international level. It follows that a deep understanding of the law requires more than technical legal knowledge: it requires an awareness of the place of law in society, and the forces that are constantly modifying the law. While our main subject is the legal system itself, we have tried to give our readers at least a glimpse of these broader influences that serve to shape the law.

Richard Chisholm

June 1992 Garth Nettheim

Preface to the First Edition

Law has always had a fascination for many people, but it has always been something of a mystery too. Many of its aspects are forbidding; the ancient buildings and traditional wigs and gowns, the costs and the delays, the strange language and extraordinary behaviour of its practitioners, the inexplicable references to long dead judges and long forgotten times in resolving problems of the last quarter of the twentieth century. Lawyers have done little to make their craft more intelligible to ordinary people, and it is hard for many people to avoid a sneaking suspicion that some of the rules and customs might, if the truth were known, be as incomprehensible for lawyers as for others.

There are reasons to believe that this situation will not continue indefinitely. Social scientists and others cannot be held at bay forever; for some time they have been asking difficult questions about such matters as the effectiveness and justification of the criminal law, and testing some of the long-held assumptions of lawyers about human responsibility and the decision-making processes of judges and juries. And the public is perhaps a little less mesmerised by lawyers' magic these days. There are worried murmurs about the alleged necessity for traditional conveyancing (land transfer) techniques in an age of computers, about such restrictive trade practices as the prohibition on lawyers advertising and the rule that a senior counsel must appear with a junior (who is paid two-thirds the fee of the senior), about the relevance of ancient legal rules and procedures to such urgent problems of the modern world as pollution, over-population and exhaustion of the world's resources.

This book has a little to say about these central issues facing the legal system; but overall it is rather a traditional book. It is designed for those who want to know something about how our legal system works. It describes as simply as possible the way laws are made, what the courts do, what lawyers do and some other features of our legal system, and it suggests further reading. We would have liked to include some other chapters, for example on legal education or the police, but enough is enough. James Thurber tells a nice story of the little girl who was given a large book on penguins by her mother;

when asked what she thought of the book, she said, after due consideration, "It told me more about penguins than I wanted to know."

Law cannot serve the community properly if it is shrouded in mystery, and there is no good reason why it should be. Much of the law is common sense, and much of it is nonsense, and you don't have to be a lawyer to recognise either. Law and lawyers should be subject to public scrutiny just like other institutions and professions, and the lack of public understanding and criticism (in many ways fostered by lawyers, however unwittingly) has been bad for both the law and society. In the trial of D H Lawrence's book, *Lady Chatterley's Lover* in 1960 a prominent English barrister asked the jury if it was the kind of book they would allow their servants to read. Many people have laughed at that story, and they are surely right: the law can do with such laughter. And so we have not always refrained from criticising aspects of the legal system, as there is a great danger, even in an introductory book, that a bland and "objective" description may give the impression that all is as it should be. This is not true, and a reader approaching the system for the first time should not be allowed to think it is. If he suspends his critical judgment until he is an expert lawyer, it may be too late.

We collaborated closely in writing this book, and, as lawyers say, we accept "joint and several responsibility" for it. In other words, I wrote the good bits, and he wrote the rest.

Richard Chisholm

December 1973 Garth Nettheim

1
Introduction

The Legal System: First Glimpses

Law, like happiness, poverty and good music, is different things to different people. Politicians may see it as the expression of current government policy, accommodating the recurrent tensions between such groups as trade unions and management, conservationists and developers, and so on. New migrants, on the other hand, may see it as unknown and threatening, a part of the "culture shock" they are suffering in their efforts to adapt to the new community, requiring them to comply with standards of conduct which are unfamiliar to them. Alternatively, they may assume the Australian law will embody what they regard as fundamental values, and that the behaviour of courts and officials will be similar to what they are used to in their home countries. These assumptions may well turn out to be quite wrong. Lawyers, by contrast, may see law as a familiar tool, to be manipulated to get the best results for their clients. Poor people may see the law as hostile and inaccessible. Rich people may see it as something they employ their tax advisers to outwit, or which protects them from the forces of violence and disorder. Police officers may see it as the source of their power and the central fact of social life. Middle class parents may see it as a damn nuisance, always requiring them to sign something and have it witnessed.

It is not surprising that the law appears in so many guises and disguises. In fact, it performs a wide variety of functions, and impinges on people's lives in many different ways. We begin by illustrating this.

Law sometimes tells people what they must do, or refrain from doing. The law says you must not steal — if you are caught doing so you can be convicted of a crime and punished. Other people and groups also tell you what you should do, although they need not always say so in the same fashion. You may be snubbed by your friends if you tell vulgar jokes (or perhaps if you don't tell vulgar jokes) or if you hold the wrong political opinions. Often the law and others tell you the same thing, and often a certain kind of conduct offends against different sets of standards, for example, standards of morality, taste and courtesy. Murder is illegal: it is also immoral, vulgar and impolite. Parking in a bus stop, or in a space reserved for handicapped drivers, may be not only illegal but also selfish, dangerous and crass.

In these examples legal rules or standards overlap with social standards. But sometimes different sets of standards tell you different things, and create some difficult choices: publishing pornography may be illegal but you may think it acceptable, or it may be legal but you think it immoral. You may be required to serve in a war which you regard as immoral. Making copies of publications, television programs or computer software, may be illegal, but treated as acceptable and sensible by most people in a particular group. For members of that group, compliance with the law might cause the person to be seen as different, rigid, or uncooperative.

At times the law tells you not to do something, but does not make it a crime. If you make a contract to do something, and fail to do it, you do not commit any offence so as to face punishment. However, the law may force you to keep your word, or order you to pay money to compensate the other person. This is "civil" as distinct from "criminal" liability.

Law sometimes tells you what to do *in order to do something else*. It is up to you to decide whether you want to lease a house or make a will; the law merely says that if you want to do these things, you have to do them in a certain way, for example by a written document. If you fail to comply with the law about making leases, or making wills, you will not achieve your objectives, since the intended legal consequences will happen only if you comply with the legal requirements.

INTRODUCTION

The law gives people powers. The police officer and the judge and the inspector from the council all owe their legal power to the law: the law authorizes them to do their jobs, and allows them to call in power if necessary. Of course, power exists in the community in many forms, and only some of them are derived from law. Important people, influential groups and big strong men all exercise forms of power which have nothing to do with the law. But organized power is, in our society, very much in the hands of the "authorities". When the judge orders you to pay a fine, or to go to prison, he or she has the police force to make you comply if you resist. In a sense, the organization of our society (like many others) is based on the notion that the state, through its legally authorized bodies, has a monopoly on organized force.

The legal system is not just rules, though rules form an important part of it. It includes legal institutions like courts, prisons, law schools, administrative offices, law libraries, parliament and lawyers' offices. It also includes people who, in one way or another, make the law the centre of their professional life: judges, magistrates, solicitors and barristers, law teachers, and so on.

The law affects people in all sorts of ways. You may find yourself actively involved in court proceedings as a member of the jury, or as a defendant to a criminal charge, or as a person (called the plaintiff) seeking damages for a motor car injury, or as a witness. However, you may also be involved in less dramatic ways. If you live in a house, whether you own it or rent it, you are involved in the law of contract and real property, and you will be affected by statutes such as the *Real Property Act*, the *Stamp Duties Act*, the *Local Government Act*, and others. If you are employed, your rights against your employer and your duties at work, your entitlement to leave and workers' compensation, your wages and conditions of work, will all be affected by the law as well as by your abilities, motivation, and your trade union.

Birth, death and marriage all require certificates, and all have important legal consequences. When you ride on a bus you enter into a contract, and you acquire rights and duties under the contract, even though it is never mentioned. When you make a will you create legal rights, at your death, in the beneficiaries. When you commit a crime you entitle police officers and sometimes even ordinary citizens to arrest you, and you entitle a judge or magistrate to punish you. When you get married you create a whole set of rights and duties between you and your new family; you may punish your children, but you must support them and send them to school.

In a sense, therefore, law is a pervasive influence in everyone's life, but that is not to say that they think about it much as they go about their affairs. Most laws fit easily into the normal framework of people's conduct and expectations. For example, most of the criminal law penalizes conduct which some people would not dream of committing because it would strike them as immoral, or stupid, or unkind, or undignified; its legal implications are scarcely relevant to their conduct. Similarly, people make many arrangements which are perfectly workable whether or not they are legally effective; the grocer can sue you for your debts but the bookmaker may not be able to do so. Yet most people, most of the time, pay their grocer and also their bookmaker; indeed some people regard gambling debts as "debts of honour" and pay them before their grocers' bills.

Law and Social Values

The law embodies certain values, some of them so important that they need to be discussed even in an introductory book. For example: a person is regarded as innocent until proved guilty through recognized procedures in a court; judges must decide cases on the evidence put before them and not on their own personal whims and prejudices; people have to be given proper notice of charges against them so that they can prepare their case and put it before the court. Principles such as these are regarded as essential to the just administration of law by the judges and lawyers who work within the system. Together, they form part of our "legal tradition".

But the values embodied in law, and in legal practice, are not all necessarily desirable. The legal system has been criticized at different times for embodying values that are seen as undesirable. For example, police have sometimes been criticised as being too reluctant to intervene to protect women against domestic violence: to the extent that this is true, it could be said that the legal system embodies a tradition of indifference to the rights of women to protection against violence. Some critics have suggested that this is not an isolated case, and that in various ways the law has failed to do justice to women. To take a startling and shameful example, when women first sought admission to the legal profession, the courts resisted this: although the legislation was in terms of "persons" joining the profession, the (male) judges found themselves able to hold that the word "person" did not include women!

A different example is the criticism that our legal system is very much oriented to uncompromising and expensive fights in court, with outright winners and losers, as distinct from encouraging negotiation and compromise. As we shall see later, this criticism has contributed to the development of "alternative dispute resolution", consisting of techniques of mediation and conciliation which are not a prominent feature of the common law tradition.

For some critics, therefore, some of the values embodied in the law and in the traditions of legal institutions are highly undesirable, either because they were always misguided or because they have become unsuitable to modern conditions. Our legal system embodies many values and traditions, some very old; precisely what they are, and how desirable they are, is, like much else in law, highly debatable.

It is not surprising that people have different attitudes to the law, and legal scholarship. The law is a generally stabilizing force in any society, tending to preserve the positions of the individuals and groups that make it up, and helping to ensure that social change is orderly and controlled. This will naturally be seen as an advantage by people who (like most lawyers in our society) occupy privileged positions and believe that the society is basically a good one. Such people tend to see "law reform" as involving only minor changes, bringing bits of the law up to date and helping it work smoothly. People who think that society is fundamentally unjust see the law very differently. From their point of view, the law stands in the way of the major changes which are needed, and supports and gives respectability to a social structure which is unjust and oppressive.

We have stressed the close relationship between law and society because it is all too easy to think that a legal system necessarily embodies "justice", or is somehow beyond politics. It doesn't and it isn't. A legal system that deals fairly between individuals and groups, and between the state and the citizen, is unlikely to be found in a society that is unjust. Law does not come down from the sky, or exist in a vacuum; it is one of our social institutions, and reflects the society in which it operates.

An example may be useful. Our legal system did not recognize any rights of the Aboriginal people to land, and it thus reflected the power of the first white invaders and their contempt for the civilization they so nearly destroyed. Through much of our subsequent history, the law reflected the prevailing views of those in power regarding Aboriginal people, especially the assumptions that they were inferior and would die out. These assumptions were at the heart of many of the laws and policies which sought either to confine Aborigines to separate areas, "reserves", or to allow them to merge with the white community. The report of the 1991 Royal Commission into Aboriginal Deaths in Custody shows how this long legal, political and social history continues to have tragic consequences right up to the present time.

Especially since about the mid 1960s, there appears to have been an increasing awareness of the terrible history of Aboriginal people since the white conquest, and an increasing willingness on the part of non-Aboriginal people to listen. By such protests as the famous "tent embassy" in front of Parliament House in Canberra in 1972 and by a variety of other means, Aboriginal people have begun to teach the non-Aborigines about the oppression that exists. Through the efforts of Aboriginal and non-Aboriginal people in such diverse areas as education, health, law and the creative arts, non-Aboriginal people are gaining a new understanding of Aboriginal people and their rights. Aboriginal people are demanding justice, and part of this demand is the right to continue as an identifiable race, to pass on their traditions and culture to the next generations. Government policies of self-determination for Aboriginal people are emerging, to be translated into legislation for land rights, and there is increasing support for Aboriginal organizations such as the Aboriginal legal and medical services. Enormous problems remain, and there is often a wide gap between government policy statements and actual programs. But perhaps we can say that the long legal and social traditions of indifference to and ignorance of Aboriginal people are coming to an end, providing the conditions for genuine progress. Legal recognition of Aboriginal claims to land, the operation of anti-discrimination laws, and other legal developments reflect these remarkable changes.

Law and Society: A Complex Interaction

This example, then, shows that the law reflects society and its values, and that changes in society can lead to changes in the law. We could say that society gets the laws it deserves. But this is not the whole story. It is misleading to talk about social values as if "society" were a single thing. People in a society have conflicting interests as well as common interests, and the institutions of society, including its laws, do not merely represent what individuals have in common. They also reflect conflicts and competition between individuals and groups and tend to protect and advance the interests of the more powerful, often at the expense of those less able to press their claims.

There is another reason why it is not enough to say that the law embodies social values: namely that the law itself appears to influence social values and attitudes. A law that acknowledged Aboriginal claims to land could play a part in influencing the way Aboriginal people are perceived by other people. Laws that require private swimming pools to be fenced, or children to wear seat belts in motor vehicles, could contribute to an increased social concern for children's safety. Laws that prohibit certain forms of discrimination, or statements that vilify people of a particular race, could influence a society to give greater respect to the rights of minorities.

Such developments may be intended (or at least welcome) consequences of the laws in question. The law may however influence social values in more subtle ways, and ways which may or may not be desired. Feminist writers, for example, have argued that the law embodies male-dominated interests and attitudes. The most striking example, perhaps, has already been mentioned, namely the decision of the courts in the nineteenth century that women were not "persons" and could therefore not become members of the legal profession.

Another commonly cited example is that for many decades the standard of responsibility in negligence was that of "the reasonable man". Of course, it can be said that in this case "man" is intended to include women. But it has been argued that in practice the application of this standard has tended to give more weight to things that generally matter to men than things that generally matter to women. More subtly, it has been argued that a word such as "reasonable", emphasising rationality, may reflect a male perspective: for women, relationships and emotional matters may play a larger part.

Although these examples lie in the past, it has been argued that some of the basic notions in the law continue to play a subtle but perhaps powerful role in contributing to a legal system that may be superficially neutral between men and women but is in fact far from neutral. Thus a leading feminist writer, Catharine MacKinnon, has written

> I propose that the State is male in the feminist sense. The law sees and treats women the way men see and treat women.

Naturally, such views provoke much debate, and there is a vigorous recent literature on this fascinating and complex topic, as can be seen from the Reading Guide at the end of this book.

As the above paragraphs indicate, some legal literature raises important questions about the relationship between law and the society, and about the nature of law. Some of this writing, such as the work of those identified with the "Critical Legal Studies" movement, has been regarded by some as exciting (or disturbing) because it suggests that many of the established ways of thinking about law are in fact distorted and unrealistic. Indeed, the traditional approaches are seen as politically biased, reflecting views and perceptions of what is "normal" and "obvious" that are not at all neutral, but are associated with a "liberal" ideology. Because these values are embedded in the ordinary language and concepts of the law, say these critics, a conventional description of the law can conceal its underlying values and make it difficult to conceive of radically different forms that a legal system might take, and arguably should take.

The range of such theoretical writing about law is very wide, and much of it draws heavily on other disciplines, including history, sociology, politics and philosophy. Some writers approach the legal system with some of the measuring techniques developed in the social sciences: they examine the operation of legal institutions as social institutions. For example, they examine the behaviour of police to see if certain types of people are more likely than others to be arrested; they examine sentencing patterns to see whether ugly people are given more severe sentences than good-looking people; they see whether people who have regular experience with litigation do better than those having their first day in court; they examine the practice of business people to see the extent to which they rely on trust and informal arrangements rather than legal contracts. The results of such research can draw attention to unanticipated consequences of law, or the gap between the aspirations and the actual achievements of different laws.

Other writers apply economic approaches to law, asking whether courts and other institutions are efficient, or cost-effective; and analysing the sorts of choices created by different forms of legal rules. Yet others analyse the way legal categories and concepts are used, and attempt to identify and criticize the values and assumptions involved.

Our Approach

In approaching this fourth edition, we reconsidered the question whether to discuss this body of theoretical literature. We have decided to maintain the more modest objectives of earlier editions. We have concentrated, therefore, on legal techniques and institutions, and have tried to explain what they are intended to achieve, and how they work, or fail to work. In doing so we have tried to be realistic rather than idealistic or naive, but we do not claim to have dealt fully with the theoretical issues involved in putting the law in its social and political context. On the whole our presentation of the law will introduce the reader to the institutions, language and concepts familiar to lawyers. It is no more than a start, and we will be delighted if readers go on to develop their understanding by further study, whether it be of particular areas of law, or of theoretical work that leads them to question familiar ways of looking at the law, including the perspectives taken in this book. Our objective is to provide all readers, whether or not they proceed further, a readable and useful account of one important part of our society, namely the legal system.

There is a large debate about the precise definition of words like "law", and "legal system", and some books start by looking at different possible definitions. However we start by simply identifying the law as comprising **those rules which will be recognized and enforced by the courts**. The aim of the initial chapters is to clarify where such rules come from in our legal system.

2
Aboriginal Law, English Law, Australian Law

Aboriginal Law

Australia has been populated for at least 40,000 years and possibly for much longer. But, for the most part, the legal system that operates today arrived with the First Fleet a mere two centuries ago.

And yet the previous inhabitants, the peoples known today as Aborigines and Torres Strait Islanders, had legal systems of their own. In his 1971 decision in the *Gove Land Rights Case* Justice Blackburn made the following comment in regard to the Yirrkala clans in the Northern Territory:

> The evidence shows a subtle and elaborate system highly adapted to the country in which the people led their lives, which provided a stable order of society and was remarkably free from the vagaries of personal whim or influence. If ever a system could be called "a government of laws, and not of men", it is that shown in the evidence before me.

The laws of Aboriginal and Torres Strait Island peoples are not merely matters of history. In many parts of Australia they continue to this day. But the settlers of 1788 and afterwards largely ignored the local laws and the rights that people had under those laws, particularly rights to land.

Within a very short time, as historian Henry Reynolds notes in *The Law of the Land* (1987), it had become obvious to the first British settlers that Aboriginal people had very definite rights in relation to particular territory. In contrast, however, to the practice in British settlements in North America, New Zealand and elsewhere, the governors of the Australian colonies never negotiated treaties for the purchase of Aboriginal land. This was in spite of some insistence from London in the early nineteenth century that Aboriginal land rights should be recognized.

To some extent the refusal to recognize Aboriginal ownership was suggested by the fiction that the Aboriginal people did not exist, that the land was "terra nullius" (a Latin phrase meaning "no one's land")!

Indeed, Governor Phillip and his officers on the First Fleet had been given to understand that Australia was virtually uninhabited. Sir Joseph Banks, who had visited the east coast with Captain Cook in 1770, had told a British parliamentary committee that there were only scattered groups of people along the coast. The first settlers were apparently surprised to discover that the population was quite large and extended into the interior of the country.

The intimate relationship between Aboriginal people and land was relatively easy to perceive. Other aspects of Aboriginal law were not as evident. And even if the Aboriginal legal system had been understood, it would not have served the need of the newcomers.

When the English settlers colonized Australia, naturally they applied the only law they knew, English law. And so, the Australian legal system — including the laws themselves, the procedures, the institutions, the values and traditions, and the legal profession — is essentially that of English law, slightly adapted for Australian conditions.

The relevant law was taken from the following principle set out by a celebrated eighteenth century lawyer, Blackstone:

> If an uninhabited country be discovered and planted by English subjects, all the English laws then in being, which are the birthright of every subject, are immediately then in force.

English law drew a distinction between "settled" and "conquered" colonies. In conquered (or ceded) colonies, the existing law remained until it was expressly altered by England. In settled colonies, which were "desert and uninhabited" there was a sort of legal vacuum, and English law applied automatically to fill the vacuum. In applying the above statement of Blackstone, the Englishmen of the time took Australia to be a settled colony.

The trouble with this view was the embarrassing presence of Aboriginal people and their nomadic and unfamiliar, but highly sophisticated civilization. But, it was thought, they did not cultivate the soil and they had no fixed habitations.

Cook in 1770 had been impressed by the apparent quality of Aboriginal life. And some of the early settlers showed genuine interest in, and sympathy for, Aboriginal people. But a majority of settlers seemed to hold negative attitudes. The Rev Samuel Marsden held that: "They are the most degraded of the human race and never seem to wish to alter their habits and manner of life". Judge Barron Field conceded they were "not absolutely hideous", and "they do not imitate humanity so abominably as the African negroes... their heads are not dog-like; nor are their legs baboonish". On this view of Aborigines, the legal consequences are not hard to guess. Individually, they were "incapable of being brought before a Criminal Court, either as Criminals or as Evidences [witnesses]... the only mode at present when they deserve it, is to pursue and inflict such punishment as they may merit". (Deputy Judge Advocate Atkins). Collectively, they had few rights: over the land, they had "a right of occupancy only", for the "right of pre-emption of the soil, or in other words the right of extinguishing the Native title, was exclusively in the government... " (Sir George Gipps). In the words of L A Whitfield, from whose *Founders of the Law in Australia* these quotations are taken:

> The implementation of this theory in New South Wales led to acts of retaliation by those who were deprived of the land where they had lived and won their livelihood. This led to repression, official and unofficial, and the pattern of attack and counter attack, murder and massacre, continued with varying degrees of intensity throughout the whole period of the encroachment by settlers on land occupied by Aborigines.

To put it briefly, Aboriginal society which had inhabited Australia for some 40,000 years, together with its legal system, was totally displaced by the society and laws of the newcomers. It was also totally subordinated to the laws of the newcomers. The issue was squarely presented in the Supreme Court of New South Wales in the case of *R v Jack Congo Murrell* in 1836. An Aborigine was charged with the murder of another Aborigine. His lawyer argued that he was not subject to Australian law. The argument, as summarized in the law report, was as follows:

> This country was not originally desert, or peopled from the mother country, having had a population far more numerous than those that have since arrived from the mother country. Neither can it be called a conquered country, as Great Britain was never at war with the natives, nor a ceded country either; it, in fact, comes within neither of these,

> but was a country having a population which had manners and customs of their own, and we have come to reside among them; therefore in point of strictness and analogy to our law, we are bound to obey their laws, not they to obey ours. The reason why subjects of Great Britain are bound by the laws of their own country is, that they are protected by them; the natives are not protected by those laws, they are not admitted as witnesses in Courts of Justice, they cannot claim any civil rights, they cannot obtain recovery of, or compensation for, those lands which have been torn from them, and which they have probably held for centuries. They are not therefore bound by laws which afford them no protection.

But the three judges of the Supreme Court ruled against him, asserting British sovereignty and holding that Aborigines were subject to British law. (A similar argument was put 140 years later, in the case of *R v Wedge*, before a single judge of the Supreme Court of New South Wales, but he felt bound to follow the earlier precedent of the Full Court.)

The modern legacy of these early attitudes and events has various dimensions; one can trace them in the high rates of poverty, illiteracy, unemployment, illness and child mortality, of Aboriginal people today; or in the resentment and alienation felt by many Aborigines who can neither find a place in white society nor pick up the pieces of their own shattered culture; or in the stirrings of guilt and the still uncertain beginnings of remedial action on the part of the white community; or in the growing assertiveness by Aborigines working through the institutions of white society (including the law), and also "going international" by establishing links with indigenous peoples elsewhere in the world, and pressing their claims before international agencies and world opinion.

The *legal* effects, however, have seemed quite clear. In particular, it was held in the *Gove Land Rights* case in 1971, on the basis of earlier judicial statements, that Aboriginal people had no rights to land except such rights as might be given under Australian law. Some Australian Parliaments have moved to restore some land to Aboriginal ownership. Several Australian Houses of Parliament have also acknowledged prior Aboriginal ownership in resolutions, or in preambles to Acts.

In June 1992 the High Court of Australia delivered judgment in the case of *Mabo v Queensland* which completely overturned the legal proposition that any land rights which Australia's Aboriginal peoples might have had were completely displaced by the British sovereignty and British law. In holding that the people of Murray Island in the Torres Strait continued to be the owners of their lands (unless and until their title was validly extinguished by government) the High Court brought Australian law on this matter into line with that of Canada, the United States and other former British colonies. The Court ruled firmly that the notion of "terra nullius" had no application to bar recognition of the property rights of indigenous peoples. Contrary statements by judges in previous times were said to be incompatible with contemporary standards of international and national law on human rights and racial discrimination.

The relationship between Aboriginal peoples and Australian law presents issues in a range of areas apart from that of land rights. The Australian Law Reform Commission in 1986 published a report recommending recognition of Aboriginal law in a range of areas, for example, recognition of traditional marriages for a number of purposes. The 1991 final report of the Royal Commission into Aboriginal Deaths in Custody made 339 recommendations in a range of areas from the design of police cells to matters of employment, housing and, indeed, Aboriginal self-determination. In the same year the Commonwealth Parliament established a Council on Aboriginal Reconciliation to seek solutions to outstanding issues in time for the centenary of Federation in 2001.

We have dwelt on this aspect of the beginnings of English law in Australia because such phrases as "the birthright of every subject" can easily mask the plain fact that our legal system began with the brutal taking of Aboriginal land without compensation, and the wholesale destruction of their society. And the first lawyers, like lawyers of other ages, with their imposing and sonorous language and eminent position in the white community, were simply men with their bags of legal tricks and traditions, who shared the vision, and the blindness, of their time.

Application of English Law in Australia

The position is rather complicated and technical, but we will present it as simply as possible: the outlines are necessary to understand the present legal system in Australia.

1. "Received" English law

The first settlers brought with them, as invisible baggage, all English law (legislation and case law) which was applicable to Australia at that time; thus New South Wales received, in 1788, all current applicable English law. When Tasmania was split off from New South Wales in 1825 it took with it its own share of the inherited law of England as it was in 1788. The position was clarified in 1828 when an Imperial statute (that is, a British one) specifically laid down that all applicable English law as at 1828 should operate in the two colonies.

When Victoria (in 1850) and Queensland (in 1859) were hived off from New South Wales, legislation provided that the laws of New South Wales as at the date of separation should continue to apply in the new colonies. This included the received English law as at 1828 except to the extent that it had been altered in New South Wales.

A separate inheritance of English law was accepted for South Australia as at 1836 and for Western Australia as at 1829.

This "received" law simply served as a sort of "starter kit" for the new colonies. It became a part of the local law, and could therefore be altered by the local legislature or developed by the local courts. But it was the law at 1828* which was received; later changes in English law were not automatically received; and from then on, it was up to the colonies to develop their inherited law as they saw fit. In doing so, they were entirely at liberty to differ from each other and (within limits: see Chapter 6) from England. In dealing with rules of law received in 1828* a court might have to decide (1) whether the rule of law was applicable to the colony in 1828,* as this would determine if it had been received at all, and (2) if it was, whether it had been altered by the colony's legislature. This is still the position, although of course nearly all of today's law has been developed through both the courts and the legislatures since 1828, so it is rare for an Australian court to apply a rule on the basis that we inherited it in 1828.

New South Wales and Victoria have both passed Acts to clarify which English Acts prior to 1828 should be regarded as part of the current law. Received common law rules can still crop up from time to time, however, as is shown by two cases which reached the High Court. In *Dugan v Mirror Newspapers Ltd* (1978) it was held that an ancient rule still applied in New South Wales which denied civil rights to convicted felons, including the right to sue in court. In *State Government Insurance Commission v Trigwell* (1979) the court upheld the continuing force in South Australia of a common law rule under which landowners are not liable if their sheep or cattle stray onto highways and cause accidents.

2. *Later English statutes*

The Australian colonies, which later became States, and, since 1901, the Commonwealth, have developed their own laws, and these form the bulk of the present Australian laws. British statutes enacted after 1828* did not apply *automatically* to Australia. But the United Kingdom Parliament remained supreme and could, and sometimes did, pass legislation which was intended to apply in an Australian

* Or 1829 for Western Australia, 1836 for South Australia.

colony (State), or in Australia generally, or even throughout the Empire. Such laws would override any existing law in the places where they apply, and were said to apply "by paramount force".

In law, the United Kingdom Parliament retained this power until recently, but in practice, of course, it would not pass a law for Australia except at the request of a State or the Commonwealth. There was, indeed, a "convention" or understanding to this effect, but a convention is not a rule of law, and did not interfere with the United Kingdom Parliament's legal power to pass such legislation.

As far as the Commonwealth is concerned, however, the convention that Australian request and consent was needed for United Kingdom statutes to apply was enacted as a legal rule in s 4 of the *Statute of Westminster* 1931, (UK) which the Commonwealth Parliament adopted in 1942.

Even if the United Kingdom Parliament would no longer pass unwanted legislation for Australia, some of its past "paramount force" legislation remained significant. Under the *Colonial Laws Validity Act* 1865, (UK) it was made clear that a United Kingdom statute applying by paramount force would override any "repugnant" colonial law, that is, any inconsistent law of a State. This rule prevented the State Parliaments from passing laws repealing or amending such United Kingdom statutes as the *Judicial Committee Acts* of 1833 and 1844 (dealing with appeals to the Privy Council), the *Merchant Shipping Acts*, and some others.

The same limitation also restricted Commonwealth lawmaking power, but the *Statute of Westminster* 1931, (UK), s 2, allowed a Commonwealth statute to override any inconsistent United Kingdom legislation, other than the *Commonwealth of Australia Constitution Act* 1900 (UK) and the Constitution itself. The Constitution can still only be amended in accordance with the referendum procedure in its own s 128.

In 1982 the Commonwealth and State governments finally agreed on a scheme to abolish the repugnancy rule as it applied to the States, to abolish all appeals to the Privy Council from State Courts, and to resolve other anachronistic remnants of the British connection.

This result was then achieved by a remarkable combined effort by Parliaments at three levels — State, Commonwealth, United Kingdom. First, all State Parliaments passed Acts, pursuant to s 51 (xxxviii) of the Commonwealth Constitution, requesting the Commonwealth Parliament to pass an Act, which it did. Second, the Commonwealth Parliament and Government acted, pursuant to s 4 of the *Statute of Westminster* 1931, (UK), to request and consent to legislation by the United Kingdom Parliament. Third, the United Kingdom Parliament passed the requested Act. On 2 March 1986 the *Australia Act* 1986, (Cth) and the *Australia Act* 1986 (UK), were proclaimed. The result was that Australian Parliaments and courts were finally in full control of Australian law.

The position set out above comes to this: we inherited English law in 1828. After this time, subject to exceptional cases of United Kingdom statutes applying by paramount force, Australian law has been built up by the legislatures and courts of the States and the Commonwealth of Australia.

Current developments in English case law still continue to have a direct bearing on Australia. In those areas where there is no relevant statute (or where there is a similar Australian statute), an English decision, particularly in the Court of Appeal or the House of Lords, will often be followed* by an Australian court if the matter is not already covered by an Australian decision. In practice, therefore, when points of law are argued in Australian courts, English cases are frequently referred to along with Australian ones. Since England has a much larger body of reported case law than Australia, it often happens that a point will be covered by an English decision but not by an Australian one. Canadian and New Zealand cases, and cases from other "common law" countries may also be referred to, but Australian lawyers remain more likely to use English cases.

* That is, the Australian court deliberately reaches a similar decision. This section will become clearer after you read Chapter 4.

3

Main Branches of Law

It would be possible to classify the law in many different ways, and so discover many different "branches" of law. Consider a regulation which gives to the police power to disperse a public gathering which might obstruct traffic; this could be classified as part of the law on police powers, or part of the law on highways, or part of the law on traffic, or part of the law on freedom of expression. None of these classifications is "wrong", and any one of them could be suitable. Which classification you choose depends on the purpose for which you are making the classification.

We base this chapter on some of the classifications which are most commonly used, and which seem to us to be most helpful in clarifying the legal system. You will see that a great deal of the classification depends on history; our legal system, and that of England on which it is based, is the result of many centuries of growth, and much of it can only be explained by reference to its history. Since there is a very close connection between the rules of law and the institutions which applied those rules, we will have to say something of the development of the courts as well.

National Law and International Law

We should first distinguish between international law and national law. The international legal system deals with relations between countries while the national legal system of each country mainly governs relations between people in that country.

It is easy to think of international law as relating to war and peace, control of international aggression, and the peace-keeping efforts of the United Nations. These are certainly matters which may involve international law, and are perhaps the most important areas of that law, but they are also areas where international law has most difficulty being effective. For the international legal system, dealing in general with legal relations between countries, lacks some of the important features of national legal systems.

International Law has no legislature: there is no body which possesses recognized and effective authority to pass legislation which binds countries. The United Nations General Assembly has considerable influence and does pass resolutions about the rights and duties of countries, but its powers in relation to countries are very much weaker than the powers of a national Parliament over its citizens. Only the Security Council has power to pass binding resolutions in furtherance of its powers to deal with threats to the peace, breaches of the peace and aggression. Other countries incur obligations in international law only if they choose to, usually by becoming party to a treaty with one or more other countries.

Again, there is nothing in the international legal system corresponding to a police force or an army. It is true that the United Nations has some peace-keeping forces, but these are very small and have to be contributed by member nations, and can operate effectively only with the consent of the countries where they are deployed. In general, these forces cannot do very much beyond policing political or national boundaries — though that, of course can be a difficult and useful function. An operation such as the 1991 deployment of armed forces against Iraq following its invasion of Kuwait is quite exceptional.

Finally, there are no courts of the kind that exist in national legal systems. There are bodies something like ordinary courts, notably the International Court of Justice (the World Court). However, this court, like other international courts and tribunals, can in general decide cases only with the consent of the countries concerned; it is therefore quite different from national courts, in which people can be sued or prosecuted whether they like it or not.

The United Nations, and the international legal system generally are sometimes criticized as being ineffective, or not being "law" at all. It is pointed out, quite rightly, that international law did not prevent the Vietnam War or the Middle East conflicts. But there are many matters where the legal system is effective. Examples include the postal system between countries, questions of nationality and citizenship, the rights of ships on the high seas, the interpretation and force of treaties, use of the world's resources, protection of the global environment, the powers and structure of such international organizations as the United Nations itself or the International Monetary Fund, are all affected by international law.

These matters, and many others like them, may not make newspaper headlines as often as threats to world security, but in these areas international law is of considerable significance. There are, of course, rules about war and peace, and they cannot be ignored, but it is broadly true to say that since the international legal system lacks the legislatures, courts and police of national systems, and depends largely on the consent of countries, it is most workable in areas where countries see their own interests as best served through orderly co-operation with others. It is, therefore, in matters of everyday relations between countries, rather than in the anxious decisions of power politics, that international law plays its most effective part.

The major modern source of international law is agreement — the growing network of treaties between two or more countries on a host of matters. Many multilateral treaties look rather like legislation. In Australia, such international agreements do not automatically become part of the national law. But they can influence the development of Australian law. They are also important in a different way. Among the subjects on which the Australian Parliament has power to make law is external affairs, and so laws that give effect to international standards may fall within the power of the Australian Parliament, even though they deal with topics that would otherwise come within the legislative power of the States.

Human rights treaties provide a good example. Two fundamental treaties in this area are the International Covenant on Civil and Political Rights (ICCPR) and the International Covenant on Economic, Social and Cultural Rights (ICESCR). Both were drafted by the UN's Commission on Human Rights in 1954 and were ultimately approved by the General Assembly in 1966. But they did not begin to operate until ratified by the governments of 35 countries, and this did not happen until 1976. Australia ratified the ICESCR in 1975 and ICCPR in 1980. In ratifying the ICCPR, the Australian Parliament established a body, now the Human Rights and Equal Opportunity Commission, with powers to oversee acceptance of the standards of the Convention by Australian governments. Two other widely accepted human rights conventions, on Racial Discrimination and Sex Discrimination, both ratified by Australia, provide the basis for the Commonwealth Parliament's *Racial Discrimination Act* 1975 and *Sex Discrimination Act* 1984.

Some regional treaty arrangements (notably the European Community) come close to establishing entities that look like federal governments, with their own legislators, courts and bureaucracies. The process of "integrating" the nations of the European Community continues to develop during 1992.

There is an ever-increasing body of international law — treaties, conventions, declarations, and the like — which set out standards relating to matters of international concern, for example human rights, and the protection of the environment.

Conflict of Laws

In an increasingly mobile world, questions often arise involving people from different countries. A couple might immigrate to Australia from a war-torn country and have no documentary evidence that they had married; perhaps the disruption had been such as to prevent marriages being conducted according to the local law. Will they be regarded in Australia as married? Again, two visitors from Singapore might make a contract in Australia which would have been effective under the law of Singapore but would not be effective under the usual Australian law about contracts. Would an Australian court hear the case, or would it say that the disputes should only be determined by a Singapore court? And, if the Australian court did hear it, what law would it apply? Or, suppose a court in Italy deals with a dispute between two Italian businessmen and orders one to pay the other a large sum of damages; then they both travel to Australia. Will an Australian court simply enforce the Italian court's order, or will the successful businessman have to prove his case all over again? Such issues do not arise only between Australia and other countries: since the law differs between Australian States in some respects, similar problems arise in cases which have some connection with more than one State.

The law governing such questions is called Conflict of Laws, or Private International Law. It has nothing to do with international law, though, so the latter description is misleading. Questions of enforcing contracts, granting divorces, and so on, even those involving people from different countries, always come before the courts of some particular country, not international bodies, and it is for the law of that country to decide how to cope with these tricky situations. Conflict of Laws, therefore, is a part of each country's national law.

It is, however, worth noting that there is an increasing tendency for countries to agree to adopt similar rules.

The Common Law

Australia, like many other countries such as England, the United States, New Zealand and Canada, has a system of law known throughout the world as the "common law". This phrase, however, is used in a number of quite different ways. It can mean a system of law based on the English system, or rules of law created by the courts rather than by the legislature, or the rules of common law as distinct from the rules of "equity". Confused? Let us explain.

1 The "Common Law" as a type of legal system

In this sense the phrase refers to the entire system, with its values, principles, institutions, procedures and rules, which was developed in England and passed on to many other countries throughout the British Empire. While there are important differences between the legal systems of Canada, Australia, New Zealand, and the United States, all these countries have based their systems on the English model, and they can be (and are) referred to as common law countries.

There are, of course, other systems. Perhaps the most important is the "Civil Law". This was originally derived from Roman law, and is the system in force in many countries in Western Europe and Latin America. It has since been adopted in Japan, Thailand and elsewhere. Even in common law countries, there are sometimes traces of the civil law, for example, in areas originally settled by the French, such as the Canadian Province of Quebec and the American state of Louisiana. Scottish law, too, is partly civil law.

Other systems include Islamic law, Hindu law, Communist law and customary systems such as Aboriginal law. (Professor Weeramantry provides a particularly lucid account of the varieties of legal systems in the first chapter of his book *An Invitation to the Law*.)

2 The "Common Law" as law created by the courts

This classification is based on the *source* of rules of law. Within the common law system of England, and of Australia, the phrase "common law" is sometimes used to indicate those rules of law which have been developed by the courts, as distinct from those enacted by Parliament.

We will see in Chapter 4 that, from early medieval times, the royal judges took over a body of rules derived from local customs and applied them uniformly throughout the realm as law common to all. Because judicial development of law was such a characteristic feature of English law, the system itself was called the common law system.

Since medieval times, however, more and more English law has been laid down in the form of legislation, by Parliament or its delegates. Sometimes legislation has enacted new rules or even new branches of law; sometimes it has simply modified or altered or added to rules developed by the judges. Parliaments, of course, have much more freedom and scope in laying down the law than the judges can hope to have: the judges must wait until a case raising a particular issue is brought before them, and, even then, their freedom of action to lay down what they think is the best rule may be limited by precedents. Thus, "common law" is sometimes used to refer to case law as distinct from legislation.

Legislation is clearly the primary source of law today. Many areas are based entirely on legislation, and even in areas still primarily based on judge-made law ("common law"), important modifications have often been made by legislation. The bulk of judicial rulings on the law today are probably rulings on the meaning of words in legislation, something we examine in Chapter 7.

3 The "Common Law" as a body of law distinct from "Equity"

This classification is less readily understood and depends entirely on the historical development of the English legal system. In this sense, "common law" means that part of English law which was created by certain courts, namely the older courts called "common law courts" as opposed to a later system of courts which administered and developed the laws of "equity". This needs some explanation.

In the late medieval period the Crown's common law courts were concerned only with certain types of topics, the main ones being — to use modern terminology — crimes, property, contracts and civil actions in "tort" (private wrongs such as trespass, nuisance, etc).

In regard to the non-criminal matters, where proceedings were instituted by an individual, the courts offered only a limited range of remedies. The principal remedies available were an order to restore property to a person, or an order to pay "damages" as compensation for some wrongful act. Private (or "civil" as distinct from criminal) actions of these types were normally commenced by a *writ*. This was a command issued in the name of the Crown, at the plaintiff's request, usually commanding the defendant to return property or to right some other alleged wrong, or give the court a good reason why not. The defendant, in order to defend the case, had to come to court and attempt to justify his or her conduct. The fact that the writ was issued in the name of the Crown — it was not just a letter from the plaintiff — indicates that the State (as we would now say) had the role of ensuring that the plaintiff's grievance was adjudicated by the courts, rather than the plaintiff having either to abandon the grievance or take some friends around and belt up the defendant. Although in one sense it can be said that civil actions are "private", they are public in the sense that the community has an interest in seeing that they are resolved according to law. The writ, in substance, survives today. In different courts it has different names, such as "summons" or "application", and it is issued by the court rather than the representative of the Crown, on the application of the plaintiff. Such "initiating process" however, continues to be an enforceable command to the defendant either to submit to the claim or come to court to defend it, and continues to embody the interest of the State in the orderly adjudication of disputes.

Returning to the early days of the common law, we find that there were many kinds of writ, and plaintiffs had to select the right one. If they chose the wrong cause of action — if, for example, they took out a writ for "detinue" when it should have been "debt", or a writ of "trespass" when it should have been "an action on the case" — the claim would fail for this reason. The choice of a cause of action would also determine what form the proceedings would take (there were differences from one writ to another) and the sort of remedy they might get.

There grew up a great deal of technical law as to the scope of the various causes of action. In fact, most of our "substantive" law about rights and liabilities developed almost incidentally to "remedial" law about the appropriateness of various types of writs. Some writs, some causes of action, had important advantages over others, for example, trial by jury instead of trial by ordeal, so that the courts allowed some of the more popular writs to expand to take over the scope of older actions.

In some situations where people felt they had suffered a wrong there was no writ available, and therefore no remedy available at common law: the common law courts recognized no actionable wrong as having been committed. There were also other situations where the judges recognized an actionable wrong but offered a remedy which, in the circumstances, was not adequate. These situations, where the law appeared defective, were to give rise to the development of equity. Despite the fact that the Crown had delegated most of its judicial work to the judges of the common law courts, it was still regarded as "the fountainhead of justice", and retained the power to adjudicate disputes between subjects. Plaintiffs complaining of wrongful conduct by another, and able to get no redress from the common law courts, could therefore petition the Crown. The Crown could receive petitions from subjects, and act on them, in situations which the judges had no power to resolve. (This remained the basis of petitions addressed from Australia and elsewhere to the King or Queen in Council and heard by the Judicial Committee of the Privy Council until 1986, when this form of appeal was finally abolished.)

Petitions were addressed by subjects to the Crown in a wide variety of circumstances. Different types of petitions were handled in different ways. For example, petitions complaining of injustices which could be remedied only by a change in the law, were considered by the Crown in Council in Parliament (the monarch and the House of Lords in the presence of the Commons representatives). Ultimately the Commons themselves took over the task of presenting most of these petitions, and this became the basis for the present legislative procedures of our Parliaments.

Other types of petitions, complaining about the inadequacy of common law causes of action, were considered by the Royal Council, and most of them were referred by the Council to the Lord Chancellor. Here we need a new heading, for it was the work of the Lord Chancellor that gave rise to the body of law known as "equity".

Equity

The Lord Chancellor was one of the Crown's leading ministers. He presided over a department called the Chancery which had begun as the Secretariat of the Council. It was the Chancery which issued the writs for common law actions, so that the Chancellor was already involved in legal work.

How did the Chancellor deal with the petitions referred to him? He could not decide them on the basis of the law, since, as we have seen, petitions were sent to him because the law was inadequate to cover the plaintiff's grievance. He decided them, instead, on the basis of "equity and good conscience", that is, on the basis of what appeared to be the merits and justice of the case. This exercise of what we would now call "discretionary" power was probably regarded as acceptable partly because the Chancellor was, until Tudor times, a leading churchman. From these beginnings there grew up a body of rules called equity, rules which were distinct from the rules of the common law, but supplementary to them.

An example can be given. A might own a farm, Blackacre, and he might want his young son C to have the benefit of it. He could, of course, simply transfer the land into the ownership of his son, but he might be worried that C would not be able to manage it properly, or might even be prevailed upon to sell it or give it away. So A might choose to transfer Blackacre to a friend, B, to hold it "in trust" for C.

The land now belonged to B, as far as the common law courts were concerned, and the possible perils or problems of C owning it were avoided. As long as B applied the land for C's benefit, everyone was happy. Generally speaking, throughout the fifteenth century, this sort of procedure worked well.

But what if B abused his trust? What if he tried to keep the profits from Blackacre for himself, or to sell it? The common law courts would not stop him: B was the legal owner of the land and could do what he liked with it. The common law refused to recognize that C had suffered any actionable wrong. All C could do was to petition the Chancellor.

This sort of thing happened so often that the Chancellors developed a set of rules to govern the situation. These rules did not directly contradict the common law rules, but avoided their effect. The Chancellors did not deny that B was the legal owner of the land. They took the view, though, that C too had an interest, an "equitable" interest, which could be enforced against B.

How could it be enforced? Not by compelling B to transfer land to C, because B was the legal owner. Not by an award of damages, for this might not be adequate. The Chancery developed special remedies of its own — in this case, it might issue an "injunction" commanding B to abide by the trust or be punished for contempt of court.

This was the origin of the modern *trust*, which forms an important part of the law today. Incidentally, it provides a lovely example of how a legal device invented for one purpose can be used for another. One of the main reasons people today use the trust is to avoid tax, and certain other consequences of owning property. Put very simply, this works as follows. B holds property (eg shares in a company) on a trust which allows B to distribute the property to any one of more of a class of people ("beneficiaries"); but B has complete freedom to decide what distribution to make, and even whether to make any distribution. None of the beneficiaries has a right to the trust property: they only have an expectation or hope that B might distribute some of it to them. Until a distribution is made in their favour, they do not have to pay tax on the property. In practice, however, they may have a very good idea of what is likely to happen, and may be able to influence it: for example B may be a relative, or a company controlled by a beneficiary. We cannot explore the details of tax law here — it is extremely complex — but we give this as an indication of the way ancient legal devices can survive and be found useful in present times.

To return to the past, the Chancellors in a similar fashion developed a number of other rules — our modern law of mortgages, for example, is based on equity. They also developed special remedies arising from breach of common law rights. For example, under the common law, breach of a contract entitled the other party to the contract to damages as compensation for the breach. But the common law would not actually force the wrongdoer to perform the contractual obligations. Equity filled the gap, by providing the remedy of "specific performance": the person was ordered to carry out the contract, and failure to do so could lead to imprisonment for contempt of court.

In time, these equitable rules became as fixed as common law rules because of the tendency, by Chancellors as well as judges, to decide cases in accordance with precedent. Equity and common law, though, remained as separate bodies of rules, administered in separate courts in England, until the 1870s. Legislation of that period, later copied in Australian States and Territories, provided for the "fusion" of common law and equity. All courts would apply principles of common law and equity to each matter that came before them; in cases where the principles were inconsistent, the equitable rules were to prevail.

In this way, then, English law recognized certain matters as being within the province of the common law courts and others as being within the province of the Chancery, and so developed "common law" and "equity" as two streams of legal rules and procedures. And this distinction was received in Australia as part of the English legal system. Even since the fusion, "equity" still exists as a specialized and identifiable body of legal rules and principles, although the distinction between common law principles and equitable principles is often blurred: now that all courts apply both sets of principles, it may not matter in practice whether a particular rule is derived from common law or equity.

Criminal Law

In discussing common law in the first sense above, we distinguished it from civil law systems. We are now using the phrase "civil law" in a quite different sense, to distinguish it from criminal law: we are talking about different parts of the English/Australian legal system.

The first and slightly surprising point is that the distinction between civil law and criminal law does not depend on any intrinsic difference in the situations dealt with by the two types of law. The same facts may give rise to both criminal and civil proceedings. If I strike you, you can either have me prosecuted by the police for the crime of assault, or sue me yourself for damages in a civil action for the tort of assault. Again, if a hotel employee takes your laptop computer from your room, he or she is probably committing the crime of larceny or theft, the civil wrong of "conversion", and also a breach of contract (another civil matter).

There is much debate among lawyers about the precise definition of criminal and civil law. Like many fundamental notions in the law, it is far from clear, but, broadly speaking, the distinction depends on the legal proceedings that may follow from the act. If the act is a crime, then criminal proceedings can be taken. They will usually be prosecuted by the police and heard in special courts (criminal courts), and they can result in conviction and punishment of the accused, who may be subjected to a penalty, such as a fine or a term of imprisonment. If the act is a civil wrong, the person injured (called the "plaintiff"), will sue the wrongdoer (called the "defendant") in a civil court seeking a remedy — perhaps an order for damages to be paid to the plaintiff (unlike a fine, which goes to the State), or an order stopping the defendant from continuing the conduct complained about. We can say roughly that criminal matters are brought by the State to punish offenders and protect the public, and civil matters are brought by persons wronged to obtain remedies for themselves.

Criminal law was at first developed by the judges, like other areas of common law, but these days most crimes are contained in statutes, which set out the offences and prescribe the penalties. The penalties prescribed are usually the maximum penalties: the court is perfectly free to set a lower one, and frequently does. It is possible, however, for the statute to prescribe a minimum penalty, or a fixed penalty, such as that of life imprisonment for murder.

Criminal law includes such matters as physical assaults, stealing or destroying property, disturbing public order, conspiracy, engaging in some kinds of "immoral" conduct, and bigamy. It also includes hundreds of smaller offences arising out of the complex relationships between people in our post-industrial society: these include traffic and parking offences, breach of licensing laws, breach of safety regulations, and many others. All these are technically a part of the criminal law, although they seldom result in people going to gaol and those who commit them are not often regarded as "criminals".

Our criminal law has a number of characteristic features. One is the "presumption of innocence". In a criminal case, persons are not taken to be guilty unless they have been proved "beyond reasonable doubt" to have committed the offence. It is for the prosecution to prove their guilt, not for them to prove their innocence. An unfortunate result of this is that a person is never proved *innocent* in a criminal case. An acquittal just means that there was at least a reasonable doubt about guilt.

Another important presumption in our system is that persons are not guilty of a crime unless they have a "guilty mind". This is a reflection of the idea that people should not be punished for what is not morally blameworthy, and also of the idea that persons should not be punished if they are not responsible for their actions. Thus people who act contrary to the law by accident, or while sleepwalking, or while insane, are not generally guilty of crimes. However, especially in many offences created by modern statutes (often but not always less serious offences), people can be guilty of crimes even though they have no guilty mind — indeed, sometimes even if they were in no way to blame for what happened. Such offences are therefore exceptions to the principle, and for that reason, among others, worry many criminal lawyers.

Another rule in our criminal law is that ignorance of the law is no excuse: you can be guilty of a crime even if you did not know it was against the law. The reason usually given for this harsh rule is the practical one that it is too easy to claim that one does not know the law; if that was an excuse hardly anybody would be convicted (except, perhaps, an occasional lawyer!).

The fact that certain conduct has been declared criminal does not mean that every person who commits such conduct will be prosecuted. Much criminal behaviour remains unknown, except perhaps to the offender, for example, many traffic offences. Much criminal behaviour is not reported, for various reasons. On many occasions (for instance, burglaries) the problem is "whodunit?" — the offender cannot be identified. And even if an offender is identified, the police may choose not to prosecute for any of a variety of reasons, for example, insufficient evidence, or the trivial nature of the offence in relation to the offender's general good character.

One last point about criminal law. In any system, it is probably necessary to have some laws to protect the public against some forms of conduct, but it is also necessary to keep those laws within reasonable limits so that they do not impose too great restrictions on the way people live their lives. It is often dangerously easy to assume that if you do not like some form of conduct you should pass a law against it. The law you pass, however, might be ineffective, or it might be so wide that most people could be convicted, or it might unfairly repress some groups in the community. The balancing of individual rights and public protection is a difficult business (see also Chapters 12 and 13).

Another aspect of the need to balance these matters is the procedure through which persons are convicted of crimes. If we gave the police unfettered power to burst into people's houses, torture suspects, and so on, they would undoubtedly catch more criminals, and if we did not insist on strict rules of evidence and procedure, courts would undoubtedly convict more criminals. But the attitude of our system has always been that it is better to allow 10 guilty people to go free than to convict one innocent person, and that there should be limits on the kinds of powers society gives to police, even at the cost of catching fewer criminals. There is, for those reasons, almost continuous debate about police powers and criminal procedure.

Civil Law

The civil (ie non-criminal) law includes both common law and equity, as well as a vast amount of law based on legislation which had no equivalent in earlier times. Civil law is far too extensive and complex to be discussed in any detail in this book. All we shall do is mention some of the major categories of the civil law. We start with two areas of law built up by the common law courts, namely tort and contract.

Torts

Tort (from the French for "wrong") was originally closely connected with criminal law, and assault is only one of many types of conduct which can be a tort as well as a crime. But the law of tort is now firmly civil and provides the plaintiff with remedies against unlawful, that is, "tortious", conduct. If the plaintiff proves that the defendant has committed a tort injuring the plaintiff, he or she can either sue for damages, or sometimes obtain an order (injunction) restraining the defendant from such conduct.

What sort of conduct is tortious? It's a mixed bag, and includes assault, interfering with others' property, defamation, allowing your dog to bite people, disturbing your neighbour with the noise of your clarinet or the smoke from your factory ("nuisance"), or indulging in some forms of unfair trade practices. Because there are these different types of claim within the general area of "tort", this area of law is often referred to as the law of *torts*, rather than tort. The bulk of cases in torts, however, involve the tort of "negligence". This covers cases where the plaintiff claims that although the defendant may have meant no harm, he or she behaved unreasonably and caused some injury to the plaintiff. The main areas of this tort are motor vehicle accidents and industrial accidents. When you are injured by someone's bad driving, you have to prove that the defendant was driving "negligently". Similarly, people injured in factory accidents have to prove that the accident arose out of the failure of the employer to take reasonable care for their safety. As with many other areas of common law, legislation has modified or replaced many rules. Thus there are statutory schemes for no-fault Workers' Compensation and, in some parts of Australia, for compensation for road accidents, which have, to varying degrees, displaced the law of torts in these areas.

Contracts

The law of contract (or contracts) deals with promises, especially commercial promises. It is designed to enforce promises, by ordering people to carry them out or to compensate the other party if they fail to do so. The law of contracts is at the heart of our commercial law, and makes many business arrangements enforceable in the courts, though it should be noted that, for a variety of reasons, most civil law disputes do not end up in court proceedings. Again, however, legislation has greatly changed things. It has modified many principles of contract law, and has in effect replaced contract law in certain areas. Even in such areas, however, the legislation sometimes incorporates or draws on ideas that can be traced to the principles of contract law previously developed and worked out by the courts.

Ecclesiastical Law and Admiralty

The common law courts and Chancery were not the only systems of courts operating in England. There were, until the middle of the nineteenth century, separate courts in England run by the Church and administering ecclesiastical law. There are still church courts which decide purely church matters. Until the nineteenth century reforms, the ecclesiastical courts had virtually sole jurisdiction in matters relating to marriage and matrimonial causes, and important jurisdiction in matters relating to wills and the estates of deceased persons. Church law on these matters was largely based on Christian canon law which had strong connections with Roman law.

In Australia today, there is a complete separation between the laws of the church and those of the State. Laws of churches may be regarded as binding by members of the church in question, but the courts apply secular law developed by legislation and judicial decision. To take a simple example, a person divorced under the secular law (the *Family Law Act* 1975, a Commonwealth law) is legally entitled to remarry. However he or she may choose to obey the doctrines of a particular religion by not remarrying, or by seeking an annulment or other procedure that is effective under the doctrines of that church.

Admiralty was another separate sub-system in English law. From Tudor times this body of law covered maritime and commercial matters, and was administered in special courts, notably the High Court of Admiralty. This body of law, too, had been ultimately derived from Roman law as applied throughout Europe by merchants and seamen. Most of the commercial law was gradually absorbed into the common law, leaving Admiralty with purely maritime matters.

Constitutional and Administrative Law

A large and important part of the law governs the structure and workings of the legal system, the system of government, and the relations between citizenship and the state. This body of law, loosely known as "public law", includes constitutional law (the nature and functioning of the Australian Constitution, and the constitutions of the Australian States) and administrative law (roughly, the laws dealing with the accountability of public officials). These areas are of particular importance because they are central to an understanding of the legal system. They are therefore discussed in several parts of this book, especially Chapters 6, 7, 10 and 12.

Other Areas

The law of torts and the law of contracts are two bodies of legal rules derived from the common law, but — especially in the case of contracts — also much affected by rules of equity. Although torts, contracts and equity constitute the major historical development of civil law, legislation has become so dominant that a large proportion of cases are determined by the application to the facts of the relevant statute. Principles of torts, contract and equity hover in the background, as it were, applying where the legislation does not deal with the problem at hand, and having a general influence on the way lawyers (and legislators) formulate and interpret legislation. Disputes arising from industrial problems are likely to be governed by industrial law, which is largely based on statute and has its own specialist tribunals; many commercial matters may be determined by legislation establishing rights for consumers, or preventing certain types of business practices. Many important areas of law, such as public health, social welfare, taxation, local government, family law, depend largely or virtually entirely on the detailed provisions of the governing legislation.

There are many different ways of classifying law. Many areas of application of the law will draw rules from different parts of the law. For example "consumer protection law" includes criminal law (eg making it an offence to publish false advertisements), licensing law (requiring those who sell firearms, for example, to have a licence), torts (claims against the manufacturer for people injured by defective products), contract (providing remedies against a shop for selling defective products), and equity (providing the basis for some remedies, such as an injunction restraining a supplier from supplying dangerous goods). And anti-discrimination legislation would prohibit suppliers for example, from restricting supplies according to a person's race, sex, or religion.

Consumer protection law is an example of a way of classifying law which has been found useful in recent times. Other examples are bankruptcy law, dealing with people who run out of money; family law, which deals with the formation, regulation and breakdown of families; succession, dealing with the fate of property when its owner dies; and such self-explanatory titles as taxation, industrial law and company law. All these areas may comprise a mixture of rules and procedures, deriving, in varying proportions, from common law, equity and legislation.

The illustration on p 35 may help to clarify some of the material in this chapter, particularly the different senses in which the phrase "common law" is used.

What appears on the third line of the illustration corresponds with Divisions of the Supreme Court of New South Wales, if we add the Criminal Law Division (and the specialist Court of Appeal for civil appeals), but it is only a sampling of the various "branches" into which it is possible to divide the Australian legal system. To give a fuller picture, we set out the classifications adopted in the monthly publication *Australian Current Law*, as a convenient series of headings under which current legal developments are reported:

1 Aboriginals and Torres Strait Islanders
2 Administrative law
3 Agency
4 Animals
5 Arbitration
6 Auction
7 Aviation
8 Bailment
9 Banking and finance
10 Bankruptcy
11 Betting gaming and lotteries
12 Bills of exchange and other negotiable instruments
13 Building and construction
14 Carriers
15 Charities
16 Citizenship and migration
17 Civil and political rights
18 Conflict of laws
19 Constitutional law
20 Consumer credit
21 Consumer protection
22 Contempt
23 Contract
24 Coroners
25 Corporations
26 Courts and judicial system
27 Criminal law
28 Damages
29 Deeds and other instruments
30 Defamation
31 Defence

32 Dependencies
33 Education and research
34 Employment
35 Energy and resources
36 Entertainment, sport and tourism
37 Environment
38 Equity
39 Estoppel
40 Evidence
41 Family Law
42 Foreign relations
43 Guarantees and indemnities
44 Highways, streets and bridges
45 Industrial Law
46 Insurance
.47 Intellectual property
48 Leases and tenancies
49 Legal practitioners
50 Limitations of actions
51 Liquor
52 Local government
53 Maritime law
54 Media and communications
55 Medicine
56 Mental health
57 Mortgages and securities
58 Negligence
59 Partnerships and joint ventures
60 Perpetuities and accumulations
61 Personal property
62 Police and emergency services
63 Practice and procedure
64 Primary industry
65 Prisons
66 Product liability
67 Professions and trades
68 Public administration
69 Public health
70 Real property
71 Receivers
72 Religion
73 Restitution
74 Sale of goods
75 Social welfare and services
76 Statutes
77 Succession
78 Superannuation
79 Taxation and revenue
80 Time
81 Tort
82 Trade and commerce
83 Transport
84 Trusts
85 Voluntary associations
86 Water
87 Weapons and dangerous goods
88 Weights and measures
89 Workers' compensation

MAIN BRANCHES OF LAW

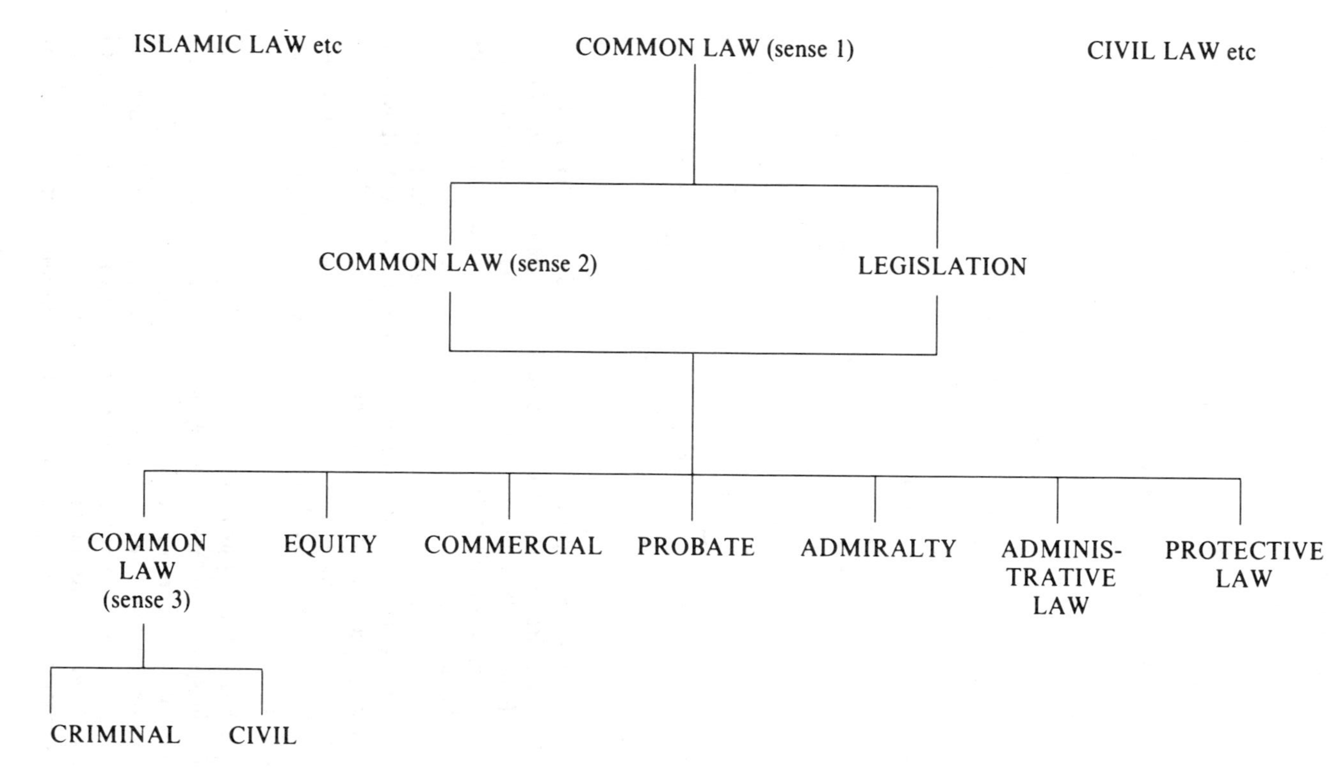

4

Where Law Comes From: Case Law

Some people are surprised to hear it suggested that judges make law. They say: "But aren't judges supposed to decide cases *according to law*? How can they also be free to create it?" They might go beyond their surprise and add: "Who are judges to make law, anyway? Law should be made by the elected representatives of the people in Parliament. Judges are not elected, and they should stick to their job of applying the law and leave the creation of new law to those who can be voted out of office if they don't do it well." This is an understandable view, but before we jump into the debate about whether judges *should* make law, let us look at how, in fact, they do so.

An Historical Approach

Parliament as we know it today began to emerge only in the latter part of the thirteenth century. Prior to this time the King would occasionally lay down law on a particular matter but, for the most part, people's affairs were governed by custom. If you wanted to know your rights in regard to the land you occupied, or your obligations to your feudal lord, or what was required in buying a cow or getting married, you would find the answer in the custom of the community. If a dispute arose, it would be decided on the basis of custom as declared by your neighbours in the communal assembly or the feudal court.

By the thirteenth century things were changing. Many of the more important disputes now came before the King's justices who were becoming specialist, professional judges. They, too, decided cases in accordance with custom, except in the relatively rare instances where there was a statute dealing with the matter, but they applied the same main principles uniformly in all parts of the realm. The law was thus made common to all parts of the kingdom — this may be the origin of the phrase "the common law".

Often, however, a new situation, not covered by custom, would come before the judges. Yet the judges were required to decide the case, and they would normally do so by applying to the new situation what they thought was the most appropriate customary rule, even though it had not previously been applied to that situation. Eventually, almost the whole body of custom became embodied in judicial decisions. New decisions for new situations continually added to the stock. Written reports of these decisions have been kept for centuries.

No one challenged the right of the judges to extend old rules to new situations by analogy or even, occasionally, to make entirely new rules. There was little feeling before the fifteenth century that the development of the law was a matter for Parliament alone.

But how did the judges lay down rules in the course of deciding disputes? Let us take an imaginary case, set in today's world, to illustrate the process.

An Imaginary Case

The setting is a young people's refuge, a place where adolescents can find help and temporary accommodation. The refuge can only accommodate 15 people at once, but there always seem to be more young people wanting to stay. Paul and Eloise, a couple who live in the refuge and are mainly in charge, do not allow overnight visitors. They go through the refuge each night at 11 pm, and say to any visitors something like: "I'm sorry, but we don't allow visitors after 11 pm, and I must ask you to leave. You are welcome to come back tomorrow". Although nothing is ever written down the residents know that this is the rule, and usually the visitors have gone by 11 pm.

One night, some of the visitors are reluctant to leave, and Eloise has to threaten to call the police before they eventually go at about

11.30 pm. At 12.30 am, however, one of the residents discovers that one visitor is still there. He tells the others the next morning and they are furious. Why? Not simply because their own friends had to leave earlier, but because Eloise seems to have treated them *unfairly* by allowing one visitor to stay while the others had to leave. They feel a sense of injustice because, as lawyers say, "like cases should be treated alike". This is shown when they demand an explanation from Eloise. She says that the visitor who remained had become ill and could not be moved until the doctor arrived, at 1.00 am. The residents (if they believe her) say, "Ah, well, ok then. That's different". And it is — the cases of the other visitors and this visitor were not alike after all, so it was right to treat them differently.

This little story illustrates at least two features of the way in which people may make law through their decisions:

(a) Rules can emerge from the way cases are dealt with, and the reasons given for them, even though the rule may never be written down in full.

(b) The rules that emerge from decisions are incomplete: they are sufficient to decide the actual problem but may leave other situations in doubt. Thus in our story, nobody thought about whether a sick visitor would have to leave until the problem arose. What would happen if a brother or sister of a resident wanted to stay overnight? Paul and Eloise will have to decide that when it happens. (If they decide to write down the rule in a way that takes in all the situations they can think of, they will be making rules by legislation, not by case law: see Chapter 5.)

A Real Case

A suitable example is the well-known case of *R v Elizabeth Manley*,* decided in 1933 by the English Court of Criminal Appeal. Elizabeth Manley told police that a man (whom she described) had struck her with his fist and stolen money from her purse. The police investigated the matter, but it turned out that nothing of the sort had happened. She was convicted of the offence of "effecting a public mischief", and appealed against her conviction to the Court of Criminal Appeal.

At the time, there was no such crime as "effecting a public mischief" on the statute books. There were a couple of old decisions

---

* This is the most common title for criminal cases. "R" stands for "Rex" or Regina", that is, the Crown. The letter "v" stands for "versus". The title reflects the idea that the state, represented by the Crown, is bringing the proceedings against the person charged. Civil cases, on the other hand, are typically titled, for example *Smith v Jones*. Curiously, lawyers use the word "and" when they are speaking of the case: they write *Smith v Jones* but say "Smith and Jones".

that a *conspiracy to effect a public mischief* was an offence, but a conspiracy is an agreement, and the law sometimes treats as unlawful a *combination* of people agreeing to do something, even though the same act done by an individual would have been lawful. No lawyer could have advised Mrs Manley in advance that she was committing an offence. In spite of this, her conviction was upheld. The Court said, in its judgment:

> the indictment [that is, the charge] aptly describes the two ingredients of public mischief, or prejudice to the community, one of these being that officers of the Metropolitan Police were led to devote their time and services to the investigation of an idle charge, and the other being that members of the public, or at any rate those of them who answered a certain description, were put in peril of suspicion and arrest.

We saw above that a decision in a particular case, together with reasons given for it, can give rise to a rule. Therefore, it is of the greatest importance that the law, particularly the criminal law, should consist of rules of general application, whether they are created by the courts or by Parliament. If *Manley's* case merely decided that Elizabeth Manley was naughty and should be punished, it would be quite unsatisfactory; it would not adequately explain why she was being punished, and it would give no guidance to other people as to what conduct is permitted and what is prohibited. Similarly, a statute which provided: "John Smith shall be liable to life imprisonment for a political speech which he made in 1991" might be a valid and effective law, but it would violate our fundamental ideas of what a law, certainly a criminal law, should be. A typical example of the form of a criminal law is our "litterbug" statute in Chapter 5. This specifies certain conduct ("Any person who throws litter in the street") and then prescribes the legal consequences ("shall be liable to a fine not exceeding fifty dollars"). The courts, too, decide cases on the basis of rules of general application, and this is the essence of the idea of decision according to law, not according to whim or prejudice.

The rule in *Manley's* case could be formulated as follows: "Any person who puts police to investigation of a false charge (fact 1) and thus exposes innocent persons to the risk of prosecution (fact 2) is guilty of the offence of public mischief (legal consequence)." This rule or principle (the technical term is *ratio decidendi*, meaning "reason for deciding") covers not only Elizabeth Manley, nor women who falsely report stolen purses, but any person who commits the sort of act she did. It is the *ratio decidendi*, or rule, which later courts use when they treat the decision as a precedent.

You Be the Judge

Perhaps the best way to grasp how judges use precedents and make decisions is to try it yourself. So assume that you are a judge, concerned with the (imaginary) case of *R v May Jones*. Assume also that the only relevant precedent is *Manley's* case.

The facts of our imaginary case are these. Mrs Jones is doing the shopping one day and she discovers her purse is missing from her bag. She remembers that a few minutes previously she had brushed against a man in the street, so she immediately reports the matter to the police, describing the man. The next day a store telephones her at home and tells her that she had left the purse on the counter. She tells the police, who are very annoyed. She is subsequently charged and convicted of effecting a public mischief and fined one hundred dollars. She appeals, and the case comes before you.

At first you think the case is a simple one; Mrs Jones has put the police to the investigation of a false charge and exposed innocent people to the risk of prosecution, and therefore, seems to come squarely within the rule in *Manley's* case. However, being a careful judge (and listening to the arguments of counsel — the barristers) you realize that the case is rather different from Manley. Mrs Jones may well have been careless and thoughtless, but it was only a mistake. On the other hand, Elizabeth Manley had told the police that a man had punched her and taken her purse, and she could hardly have made a mistake about that. When you check the report of *Manley's* case, you see that the trial court referred to people who make charges "entirely bogus to the knowledge of those making them". That clinches it: the cases are different, and the difference is that Mrs Manley told a deliberately false story, but Mrs Jones just made a mistake.

Let us leave you there for a moment. You know the facts, and you know the relevant precedent. How will you decide the appeal? Should Mrs Jones be convicted or acquitted? We suggest that you think about it for a while before reading on.

****

Well, you have decided. How would a judge decide? Here is an imaginary decision of an appeal court consisting, as is usual, of three judges. The judgments are a little simpler and shorter than most real judgments, but they illustrate the kind of reasons judges might give in such a case as this.

Justice White: The *ratio decidendi* of *Manley's* case is that any person who puts police to investigation of a false charge and thus exposes innocent persons to the risk of prosecution is guilty of effecting a public mischief. The accused in the present case, Mrs Jones, comes squarely within this rule, but it has been argued that she is nevertheless not guilty of the offence because she did not tell a deliberate falsehood. I do not accept this argument. There is no reference to deliberate falsehoods in the judgment of the Court of Criminal Appeal in *Manley's* case, and the consequences of her conduct are the same whether the false charges were deliberate or accidental. The rule in *Manley's* case is not confined to dishonest reports, but includes cases such as the present, where serious allegations were made to the police carelessly, without any effort to check that they were at least likely to be true.

Finally, counsel for the accused said that a conviction in a case such as this would discourage people from co-operating with the police by reporting suspected crimes. I cannot agree with this argument either. The only possible effect of a conviction here would be that people would be more careful in making allegations to the police, which would be entirely desirable. In any case, it is not for me to consider such matters; my task is to apply the law as it has been laid down in *Manley's* case, and I find the accused guilty of the offence charged, and dismiss the appeal.

Justice Black: In this case, the accused has not been dishonest: at the most she has been careless or reckless in reporting a suspected crime to the police. Yet as counsel for the prosecution points out, there is no reference in *Manley's* case to dishonesty, and the references to wasting police time and exposing innocent people to suspicion are applicable to this case.

Nevertheless, in my opinion the rule in *Manley's* case does not extend to negligent, as opposed to deliberate, misconduct. The accused in that case was clearly guilty of a deliberate lie, and although the court does not stress that aspect, the decision cannot be taken to extend to the quite different situation of the present case.

Nor am I prepared to extend the rule in *Manley's* case. To do so would probably discourage people from reporting cases to the police unless they were absolutely sure of their facts. This would deprive the police of a great deal of the co-operation from the public on which they often depend. Furthermore, I would not wish to extend the criminal law into an area so far from what most people would consider criminal, and in a way that subjects people to the risk of prosecution for conduct which is merely careless. If the law is to be extended in that way, let it be done by Parliament, not by the courts.

I therefore hold that the accused is not guilty of the offence charged, and allow the appeal.

Justice Grey: I agree with my learned friend* Justice Black that this appeal should be allowed, and I have nothing to add to the reasons he has given. The appeal is therefore allowed, and the conviction quashed [that is, discharged: Mrs Jones is held to have committed no offence].

At this stage we can note a number of points:

1. Although all judges accepted *R v Manley* as a binding precedent, they still had to make a *choice* in order to decide the case before them. The question in *Jones'* case was different from that in *R v Manley*, and it could not be decided merely by application of the precedent. Judges are at times reluctant to admit that they have such choices, and pretend that their job involves only a mechanical application of precedent. Justice White does this at the end of her judgment. In making such choices, judges should (and do, whether they admit it or not) have regard to the purposes of the law, and to their own ideas about what is fair and just.

2. If the facts had been the same as in *Manley's* case, all judges would have convicted Mrs Jones, but where the facts are slightly different, the precedent has to be either "followed" or "distinguished". Justice White "followed" *Manley's* case, because she relied on it as a precedent and reached the same result. By following it, she broadened the law by *extending* it to negligent conduct. Justice Black "distinguished" *Manley's* case, because he admitted that it was a precedent but found that the case before him was different, and he therefore reached a different result. By distinguishing *Manley's* case, he narrowed the law by *confining* it to *deliberate* wrongdoing. If a judge is "bound" by a precedent, he or she must either follow it or distinguish it.

3. Although in such cases as this the courts do make law, the process of judicial law-making is different from legislation. Judges can change the law only by working with the cases that happen to come before them, and within the limited choices left open by previous cases. Parliament, on the other hand, can make general provisions covering wide fields, without regard to earlier cases. If it passes legislation contrary to earlier precedents, it simply wipes them out, since Parliament is a superior law-making authority to the courts.

4. Cases such as *R v Jones* or *R v Manley*, where judges make law,

* Such formal expressions of professional solidarity should not be taken at face value. The phrase "my learned friend", used in the course of a heated argument, may be used in a tone implying that the opposing counsel is really a dangerous idiot who should never have been let out of Law School.

are relatively uncommon. In most of the cases decided every day by the courts, there are no arguments about what the applicable law is. Only the facts are in dispute; whether Smith was driving over 60 kilometres per hour or whether Bloggs really has a bad back or is exaggerating it to recover greater compensation than he deserves. It is only cases like *Jones* and *Manley*, cases which change the law, that are reported in the law reports. Lawyers have no interest in a decision about Bloggs' back (a question of *fact*) because that affects only him, but they are very interested in a decision about whether the offence of effecting a public mischief can be committed negligently (a question of *law*), because that can affect everybody.

5. Many other questions could arise about *Manley's* case, and they would require some judge to go through the sort of process we have been through, and there will be a new precedent, and a new gloss on *Manley's* case. For example, perhaps the only person placed under suspicion might be a foreign diplomat, who could not be charged with an offence. Or, perhaps the police might pick up a man following a false description of a non-existent crime, and find that they have not wasted their time because they were looking for him anyway for another offence. As such cases are decided, the "rule in *Manley's* case" will become encrusted with other precedents explaining it, developing it or restricting it. Much of our law consists of such series of cases, built up like coral reefs. (Lawyers love metaphorical language. One wrote that English law was "forged slowly on the anvil of reality"; another created a curious image of a judge "going out into the thickets of decided cases, searching for his principles".) It is one of the skills of a good lawyer to trace the patterns of the hundreds of precedents, many centuries old, recorded in the law reports.

6. The subsequent fate of *Manley's* case as a precedent provides a good illustration of some of the ways the system of precedent operates. A decision only binds lower courts in the same legal system. *Manley's* case was criticized in later decisions because the very general notion of causing a public mischief, as one distinguished English judge said in 1954, "would leave it to the judges to declare new crimes". In 1974 the House of Lords in effect overruled the decision (although they suggested that on the facts Mrs Manley may have been guilty of a separate offence, namely "perverting the course of justice"). And in 1957 the South Australian Supreme Court refused to follow it, saying that there was no offence of effecting a public mischief in South Australia The House of Lords could overrule *Manley* because it was a higher Court in the English legal system, and the South Australian Supreme Court could refuse to follow it because it was a decision of a court in a different legal system.

How far Australian courts today would follow *Manley* is an open question, but we think it is likely that they would agree with the House of Lords that it should no longer be followed. Decisions which are not binding are merely "persuasive" — courts like to follow them but do not have to. How persuasive they are depends partly on the status of the court. For example, a single judge in NSW would be more willing to depart from a ruling of a single judge in Victoria than from a ruling of the Full Court of Victoria, although technically neither is binding on the NSW judge. It also depends on the quality of the reasoning. Thus when the South Australian Court refused to follow *Manley* it delivered a very elaborate criticism of the judge's reasoning in that case. Incidentally, in some jurisdictions, including the United Kingdom, parliaments have created a similar offence in legislation.

Sometimes, it is difficult to say just what the *ratio decidendi* of a case is, as judgments are often much more complex than the ones we have considered, and in some cases the decision is made by several judges, all of whom give different reasons for arriving at the same result! These and other technical questions have to be tackled by anyone wanting to understand the system of precedent in detail. More elaborate discussions can be found in the books mentioned in the Additional Reading list which precedes the index at the end of this book.

Should Judges Make Law?

One of the features which distinguishes English, and consequently Australian, law is the fact that a great deal of it is contained only in precedents. Most of the law of contracts, torts and crime is still contained in the thousands of cases which make up the bulk of modern law libraries. These cases date back for hundreds of years, and many very old cases are still good law today. (The theory is that old cases, like old soldiers, never die; but in practice — again like old soldiers — they are often conveniently forgotten.) Most other legal systems have reduced their laws into codes. For example, most of the laws of the modern western European countries are based on the Napoleonic code, which in turn is based on Roman Law. Of course, much of the law in Australia today is based on legislation, but a great deal of it still depends on decisions like *R v Manley*. Cases still occasionally arise which are quite new, and where nobody is sure what the law is, because no similar case has ever been decided.

Some people think that it would be better if most or all of our case law were put into a code. This may well be right. Three of the Australian States have enacted criminal codes. But such a change would not mean the end of judicial law-making; we will see in

Chapter 7 that even with legislation, there are lots of points that have to be interpreted by the judges, and in their interpretation they make law.

Should judges make law? If this means "should judges have to make decisions about the law in order to decide cases?" we think the answer is that they inevitably will. A system where the law is so clear that its application is a purely mechanical task seems to us to be impossible. (If you do not believe us, think up a definition of a crime which is so clear that no difficult cases, that is, cases where it has to be interpreted further, can arise.) In that sense, whoever applies law to facts will inevitably have to interpret it, and that means in effect making new law.

A more difficult question is whether the system of precedent which we have is ideal. It is *stricter* than in most other places; the notion that judges are *bound* to follow some precedents seems a distinctive feature of the common law. Even in the United States, which of course originally took its law from England, judges seem to be more flexible and willing to depart from earlier decisions than in England or Australia. Flexibility is important, because in a rapidly changing society yesterday's solutions might not be good enough. The English system is sometimes criticized for tying the judges too much to the past. This may be so, but it is also true that the system is in practice more flexible than you would think from the theory: that is one reason we started with examples rather than theory. The late Mr Justice Murphy of the High Court wrote scathingly of the doctrine of precedent: "I have managed to apply it at least once a year . . . it is a doctrine eminently suitable for a nation overwhelmingly populated by sheep".

The need for flexibility raises further questions about the competence of judges to decide "policy" issues: they are not elected, and, being mainly men, from comfortable backgrounds, and moving in a particular section of the community, their decisions may tend to reflect views and assumptions that are typical of people of such background. For this reason it is good to see judges playing some part in public affairs, such as working on law reform commissions or public inquiries; such activities can do much to help them keep "in touch".

It may be that in any system there is a need to balance certainty with flexibility. People ought to be able to know what the law is, so they can organize their affairs accordingly; therefore the law ought to be clear and unchanging. But the law also needs to adapt to changes in society, and judges should not be tied to rigid rules which would be unjust in unusual cases. The existing system of precedent represents a compromise between these objectives. Whether it is the best compromise is debatable.

We would make only one comment on this wide topic. It may be that that balance should not be the same for criminal law and civil law. Almost all criminal law was built up by the judges at a time when legislation was rare. Today, however, governments and people are very concerned with preventing crime and Parliament is constantly passing criminal legislation. Furthermore, there is a particular problem about cases which extend the criminal law. They are retrospective; that is, they punish people for acts which were not known to be crimes at the time when they were committed. A controversial case is *Shaw v DPP** in 1963, where the House of Lords convicted a man of "conspiracy to corrupt public morals" for publishing a directory of prostitutes. Most lawyers at the time had never heard of such an offence, and the House of Lords had to dig up some very old precedents, quite different from *Shaw's* case itself, to support the decision. The fact was that they were making a large development in the law, giving the courts a power as vague as the notion of "public morality".

The decision raises the same problem as *Manley's* case, discussed above. Shaw was punished for an act which was not a crime when he did it. The English philosopher Jeremy Bentham had a sharp word on the subject. Referring to judges making law, he wrote:

> Do you know how they make it? Just as a man makes law for his dog. When your dog does anything you want to break him of, you wait till he does it and then beat him. This is the way you make laws for your dog, and this is the way the judges make law for you and me.

It seems to us that judges should no longer play a significant originating part in the development of the criminal law. This view received substantial recognition by the House of Lords itself in *DPP v Withers* in 1974, the decision which overruled *Manley*. England now has a specific offence, created by statute in 1967, of causing any wasteful employment of police time by knowingly making a false report of a crime. Our imaginary Justice Black, like us, would prefer this to the rule in *Manley's* case.

* DPP stands for "Director of Public Prosecutions", an official who is responsible for the prosecution of some of the more serious crimes in England. Several Australian jurisdictions also have a DPP.

5

Where Law Comes From: Legislation

The Legislature

Under the Commonwealth Constitution, "the legislative power of the Commonwealth shall be vested in a Federal Parliament, which shall consist of the Queen, a Senate, and a House of Representatives . . . ". There are similar provisions in the States' Constitutions. For example, the New South Wales Constitution provides: "'The Legislature' means His Majesty the King with the advice and consent of the Legislative Council and Legislative Assembly . . .".

These ancient formulas give a misleading idea of what actually happens. When legislation has been passed by the Parliament, it is presented for signature (the "royal assent") by the Governor-General in the case of Commonwealth legislation and by the Governor of the State in the case of State legislation. It is a long time since the British monarch played any real role in Australian legislation, and the *Australia Act* 1986 removed any remaining possibility that the Queen would play a real role in Australian legislation: see Chapter 2.

In practice, the assent of the Governor-General or Governor is always given, since there is a very strong constitutional convention that they act on the advice of the government of the day. It is not important whether the Governor-General or Governor approves or disapproves of the legislation in question. However, one can never be too sure about these things, especially since 1975, when a Governor-General dismissed a federal government which still commanded a majority in the House of Representatives. The position is, therefore, that legislation does not become law until it receives assent; and in practice, since as we shall see legislation only passes if the government of the day wishes, assent is always given. So far.

In practice, then, the legislature for the Commonwealth is the House of Representatives (the Lower House) and the Senate (the Upper House); for New South Wales, the Legislative Assembly (the Lower House) and the Legislative Council (the Upper House), and so on. Any bill (that is, draft legislation) which is agreed to by a majority in each House* through the Parliamentary procedures, then receives the royal assent and becomes a statute, an Act of Parliament, and a part of the law. Acts of Parliament are published by the Government and can be purchased.

How Statutes Are Made

The Australian Constitutions, as mentioned above, simply speak of law-making power being vested in the Queen and the two Houses of Parliament. But if all these people were to assemble in a large hall and vote for a proposal, this proposal would not be recognized by the courts as a statute; it would not have been passed in the proper fashion.

The procedure for passing statutes has been evolved through seven centuries of practice in the British Parliament, as modified, in some respects, by statutes. The same procedures are followed in Australian Parliaments though, again, custom is modified by the terms of our State and Federal Constitutions, by earlier statutes, by standing orders of the Houses, and so on. There are differences in detail from one Parliament to another: what follows is a broad outline of standard legislative procedure.

First a note on the political background to legislation. The proposal for an Act of Parliament can come from many sources. It might have been part of the election policy of the political party which won a majority in the Lower House and so now forms the Government. It might be a matter of policy which has been adopted by the Government since it took office. It might be submitted to a Minister by one

* The Queensland Parliament, and the legislatures of the Northern Territory and the Australian Capital Territory, consist of only one House.

of the Departments. It might come from a private member of Parliament, from some outside organization or from a Law Reform Commission.

Generally speaking, wherever the proposal comes from, it will have to be accepted by Cabinet. Cabinet represents the leadership of the majority party in the Lower House, and so commands the votes of the majority. Cabinet is also responsible for organizing the business of Parliament; unless it makes a place for the bill in its legislative timetable, it will have little or no chance of success.

Normally there will be a long series of discussions about what provisions the bill should contain. These discussions will take place within the appropriate Government Department and possibly in Cabinet itself. Experts and interested outside bodies may also be consulted. If the proposal is particularly important, there may be considerable public discussion as well, in the media and elsewhere. When the main outlines have been worked out, the proposal will be sent to Parliamentary counsel to be put into the form of a statute; it then becomes a "bill", ready to be introduced into Parliament.

Now the Parliamentary procedure commences. The bill will be initiated by the appropriate Minister, probably in the Lower House by a motion for leave to introduce the Bill. After this has been agreed, the next stage is the First Reading. This, too, is a purely formal exercise; all that happens is that the title of the bill is read out, there is no debate and a day is fixed for the Second Reading.

It is at the Second Reading that the bill is debated, though the discussion will be directed to the principles of the bill, not the details. If it is not rejected at this stage, it goes on to the "committee stage". The committee may be an actual committee or, more likely, a "committee" constituted by the whole House. In committee, the details of the bill are debated, clause by clause, then the bill is "reported" back to the House together with any amendments.

Finally, the bill, subject to any amendments, is given a Third Reading, at which there may be further debate. If the majority then vote for it, it has been passed by the House. These procedures can be condensed, and it is possible for a bill to pass through several — or even all — stages in the one day.

However, the bill still has to go through the same procedures in the other House (if there is one), which will, in most cases, be the Upper House. If the Upper House rejects the bill, a "deadlock" situation arises. The different Parliaments may have special procedures for resolving deadlocks. If the Upper House accepts the bill but makes its own amendments to it, these amendments have to be considered in the first House. This, too, can lead to deadlocks, though usually agreement is eventually reached.

Once the bill has been passed by both Houses, it is ready to receive the royal assent. When this is given the bill becomes a statute, part of the law of the land. It may commence to operate from the date of royal assent or from some other date, later or even earlier, if this is specified.

This, then, is how Parliament makes law. In practice, nearly all the hundreds of bills debated each year in the Commonwealth and States are certain to be passed because they are presented by the Government, and the Government usually has the majority vote in the Lower House. The party system ensures that all Government party members, in the Lower House particularly, vote for bills proposed by the Government. Even the bills that are strongly opposed by the Opposition are usually certain of success. Except in the infrequent case of parties allowing their members a "free" vote on a particular measure, it is rare for Government members to "step out of line" and vote against a Government bill. However, a Government may be less certain of having its way in the Upper House. And minority Governments are not unknown.

Some people say that the system is a sham or a farce. If they mean that the Parliament does not consist of men and women who are free agents, making decisions and judgments according to their own lights or according solely to what they think is in the interest of the country, then they are right: but Parliament has not been like that for a long time, if it ever was. In fact, it is only rarely that Parliament actually makes decisions at all: by the time most bills are being debated, all important decisions have already been made. As Professor Sawer says in *Australian Government Today:*

> Most of the time, however, Parliamentary debate is not a process of decision, except in a formal sense. It is one of registering, defending and publicizing decisions already taken by the majority party, Cabinet and the civil service, and drawing attention to the different proposals of the Opposition. It is a continual inquest into the deeds and misdeeds of the Government, and a continual reminder to the electors that an alternative exists.

He goes on to argue that one cannot dismiss Parliament as a farce, for it serves a useful purpose in informing the public of reasons for decisions and the influences which have operated to produce them; such a source of public information about the process of Government is not available in totalitarian states. The media — newspapers and magazines, radio and television — also serve a valuable function in informing the public about the workings of Parliament, even if there is a tendency to look for sensation or scandal.

The situation may be rather different if the Government does not have a majority in the Upper House (or, more rarely, in the Lower House), or if Government party members are prepared to cross the floor and vote with the Opposition. This has often been the position in the federal Parliament in recent years, with the result that Senators have sometimes forced significant changes to Government bills and even rejected them altogether.

We cannot pursue the debate about the merits of the Parliamentary system, or the many questions about the sources of political power in the community. From a legal point of view none of these things matter: all legislation passed by Parliament in the way described above is law and will be enforced by the courts and other authorities. Even if the effective decisions are made elsewhere, by others, those decisions cannot have the force of law without the authority of Parliament. Consequently, even when Parliament is nothing more than a "rubber stamp", it is still a necessary rubber stamp.

Delegated Legislation

Parliaments, however, are not our only law-makers. To an ever-increasing extent, the affairs of society are governed, not by statutes passed by "our elected representatives, in Parliament assembled", but by regulations, rules, ordinances, by-laws and the like, made by public servants.

This is possible only as a result of the delegation by Parliament, in a statute, of some of its own law-making power. The practice has become common in all modern nations for the legislature, in passing an Act, to leave a number of matters to be worked out by some other body or individual such as the Governor-in-Council, statutory authorities, or local councils.

The Family Law Act 1975 (Cth), s 125, provides a typical example. It is as follows:

> The Governor-General may make regulations, not inconsistent with this Act, prescribing all matters that are required or permitted by this Act to be prescribed or are necessary or convenient to be prescribed for carrying out or giving effect to this Act and in particular — [then follows a list of specific topics, including for example the payment of court fees].

In such a provision Parliament has conferred on the Governor-General a broad power to make law. The Governor-General does not personally draw up such regulations, of course. They are made by him "by and with the advice of the Executive Council". And who is the Executive Council? Simply the Cabinet acting in its formal capacity. Thus, in effect, the regulation-making power is conferred by Parliament on Cabinet, that is, on the Government. In practice the regulations are normally prepared in the appropriate Government department, and receive formal endorsement by the Governor-General and the Executive Council.

Sometimes the power to make delegated legislation is conferred on an individual Minister, or a department, or local government authorities, or other individuals or bodies.

Reasons for Delegating Law-making Power

Parliament delegates its law-making power for a variety of reasons. One is sheer pressure of time. Parliament exists not only to pass laws but also to function as a forum for discussion of public affairs, for the airing of grievances and for the supervision of Government. So many matters come within the scope of modern Government that Parliament cannot hope to pass all the legislation needed. Accordingly, it tends to lay down general principles in a statute, and to leave the details to be worked out by the persons who are responsible for administering it.

But even if Parliament had ample time to legislate completely on every topic, it would sometimes lack the expertise to do so. The subject matter of much modern legislation is so complex and technical that the detailed rules can only be worked out by experts — for example, emission standards for various classes of factory chimneys.

Another reason for delegating law-making power is that it allows for greater flexibility in the law. Legislation on a new topic may be experimental in nature, or may, for some reason, need to be altered fairly quickly. The process for passing statutes through Parliament, outlined above, is cumbersome, and it is much more efficient to allow matters of detail to be governed by regulations which can be made, altered or repealed at any time.

The reason why Parliamentary legislative procedures are cumbersome is that they are designed to ensure that the law shall be made publicly, and subject to the criticism of the people's representatives. These are valuable democratic safeguards. The same cannot be said of procedures which allow laws to be made by public servants, endorsed by the Executive Council, and then announced in the *Government Gazette* without any opportunity for discussion at all.

A large number of people have been very concerned about this practice. They have accused Parliament of abdicating its responsibilities, and spoken about the decline of Parliament as an institution.

The problem has been felt in Britain, in Australia, and in other countries as well. It is a problem of reconciling legislative and administrative efficiency with democratic principles.

Supervision of Delegated Legislation

Certain procedures have now been widely adopted to ensure that Parliament can and will keep an eye on the sort of regulations that are made under the powers it has delegated.

A common requirement is for regulations to be notified in the *Government Gazette*, and then, within a specified period tabled in Parliament, where they can be disallowed by either House (not by Parliament as a whole) within a further specified time. (In Victoria both Houses must pass any resolution to disallow delegated legislation.)

This sort of procedure gives some publicity to new regulations (at least to avid readers of the *Government Gazette*). It also ensures that Parliament has an opportunity to supervise the use that has been made of the law-making power which it has delegated. Does Parliament use this opportunity?

To ensure that it does, another safeguard has been developed in the United Kingdom, Commonwealth, and all State Parliaments. This safeguard is the establishment of a "scrutiny" committee — either a committee of one House, or a joint committee from both Houses. It is the special function of such a committee to examine all delegated legislation tabled under the above procedures, and to report to the House (or Houses) any which appear to be objectionable for one reason or another. It remains open for any other member of Parliament to move that delegated legislation be disallowed by the House.

In addition, greater care is being taken nowadays to see that delegated legislation is properly drafted. Also, much delegated legislation is now made only after consultations with the organizations or persons most likely to be affected by them.

Safeguards such as these may, perhaps, slow down the making of delegated legislation. But they help to ensure that proper care is taken when public servants make legislation of this type, and that such delegated legislation will receive some supervision from Parliament.

Courts, too, may be involved in reviewing the *legality* of delegated legislation. This may happen if someone argues that there has been a failure to follow essential procedures, or that the delegated legislation goes beyond what the parliament has authorized.

Law Reform

From time to time existing law (both case law and legislation) requires reform, especially as circumstances in society change. From time to time new social needs make themselves felt requiring new law.

Until recent times Australians have left legal renewal to political and bureaucratic processes. Increasingly, however, it has been felt desirable to entrust aspects of this work to separate bodies, especially Law Reform Commissions. As the Senate Standing Committee on Constitutional and Legal Affairs noted in its 1979 Report *Reforming the Law:*

> Ministers and Departments have increasingly come to recognize the advantages of delegating significant responsibilities in the initiation and development of law reform proposals to independent law reform agencies. So too has Parliament, whose function it is to enact the legislation which ... is the only effective means of large scale law reform. Parliament itself lacks the expertise, time and resources... The Executive ... usually has much greater resources ... but still nonetheless finds it difficult or inconvenient to allocate those resources away from more immediately pressing tasks.

Stan Ross in his valuable study *Politics of Law Reform* writes:

> ... the modern era of law reform in Australia begins with the establishment in 1966 of the Law Reform Commission of New South Wales, the first full-time Commission in Australia. The New South Wales Commission is now only one of eleven such law reform agencies in Australia. All states and territories (the territories are covered by the ALRC) now have law reform agencies with Victoria having three separate bodies and South Australia two.

Other bodies than the law reform commissions are also involved in developing specific law reform proposals. They include: lawyers' professional organizations, frequently operating through specialist committees; the Law Foundations of New South Wales and Victoria; parliamentary committees; specialist standing advisory councils such as the Administrative Review Council, the Family Law Council or the Australian Institute of Criminology; ad hoc inquiries such as Royal Commissions into such matters as taxation, poverty, Aboriginal land rights, drugs, prisons and so on.

Of course, Parliaments and bureaucracies retain the power to develop their own law reform initiatives. The 10-year evolution of the federal *Freedom of Information Act* 1982, was almost entirely a matter of interplay between Ministers, Departments, Inter-Departmental Committees, the Senate Standing Committee on Constitutional and Legal Affairs and some independent-minded senators.

The work of the law reform commissions is valuable in producing thorough research and consultation leading to carefully considered proposals for law reform. The fact that many such proposals remain unimplemented is probably less a factor of the quality of the reports than a reflection on the politics and resistance to change of Parliaments and bureaucracies.

6

Limits on Legislative Power

It has been said of the British Parliament that it can do everything except make a man into a woman. It can legally pass Acts requiring all Yorkshiremen to wear red hats, or providing that the legal currency of the realm shall henceforth be clam shells, or making it a public duty to shoot children and pensioners on sight.

This is lawyers' talk, of course. There are all sorts of good reasons why the British Parliament should not, and in practical terms *could not*, pass such legislation. But these reasons would be political, based on the fact that the people would not stand for that sort of thing, and might vote the Government out of office or stage a revolution. The point lawyers make when they speak of such fanciful things is that the legal system imposes no *legal* limitations on what the British Parliament can do. As long as a statute is passed in the proper form, so that it is a statute, the courts will enforce it, whatever it says.

Of course, the theory has never been really tested, and it is conceivable that the judges would refuse to comply with outrageous legislation, or, more likely, that they would resign rather than enforce it. However, aside from such speculation, it is true that the Parliament is legally unrestricted in its power, and whatever statutes it passes will be applied by the courts. (This theory, however, requires modification as the UK becomes more fully integrated into the European Community.)

Although in many respects the Australian legal system is the same as the English, the position is quite different in relation to the legislative power of Parliament. The difference arises from the fact that legislative power in Australia is shared between the six State Parliaments and the Commonwealth Parliament. This sharing of legislative power means that no Parliament in Australia has the same degree of power as has the UK Parliament over its territory. In this chapter we look at the way that legislative power is limited in Australia.

Legal limits on legislative power require someone to enforce them, and in our system this job is done by the courts. If a Parliament, even the Commonwealth Parliament, passes legislation which falls outside its power, then the courts will declare it invalid. When this happens the legislation is ineffective and will not be enforced by the courts or other authorities, such as the police. The limits on legislative power are therefore of real importance, and quite a few important statutes have been declared invalid by the courts over the years.

Legal Restrictions on Australian Legislatures

1 Acts of the United Kingdom Parliament

The Constitutions of the States, and the Commonwealth Constitution itself, are contained in or derived from statutes of the United Kingdom Parliament. Therefore, at least in theory, that Parliament had legal power to repeal or amend these statutes, and thus change the structure of Australian constitutional law, in and way and at any time.

Apart from this, as we saw in Chapter 2, there was also a general power in the United Kingdom Parliament to pass statutes applying in Australia by "paramount force". The Commonwealth Parliament by virtue of the *Statute of Westminster* 1931, s 2* had power to override such Acts in its sphere; State Parliaments did not.

However the *Australia Act* 1986 (Cth) and the *Australia Act* 1986 (UK) both provide that the power of the United Kingdom Parliament to legislate for Australia is terminated . To prevent the United Kingdom Parliament from repealing *that* provision, the Acts specify that they may be repealed or amended only by a Commonwealth Act passed at the request or with the concurrence of the Parliaments of all the States. This is likely to be regarded in both countries as

---

* "s" stands for "section".

effective to end the United Kingdom Parliament's law-making powers for Australia.

Accordingly, this "Imperial" limitation may fairly be regarded as having historical significance only.

2 Territorial limitation

Another limitation arising from the British connection is that power is conferred on Commonwealth and State Parliaments, under their Constitutions, to make law "for the peace, order and good government" of their respective territories. This form of words has been thought to restrict the Australian Parliaments from passing laws operating outside their territories. Thus, a State law making it an offence for one French person to punch another in France would not be a valid law, simply because it could not be described as a law "for the peace, order and good government" of the State. By contrast, such a statute passed by the UK Parliament would have to be accepted as binding law by British Courts (though not, presumably, by French Courts).

This restriction is not now of great importance. The courts tend to regard as valid any law which has some connection (even a slight connection) with the peace, order and good government of the territory concerned. Section 3 of the *Statute of Westminster* 1931 (UK) attempted to make it clear that the Commonwealth, at least, had power to make laws having extra-territorial operation. Section 2 of the *Australia Act* 1986, (UK) does the same for the States.

3 The Commonwealth Constitution — apportionment of legislative power

The most important restrictions on the law-making power of Australian Parliaments arise under the *Commonwealth of Australia Constitution Act* 1900 (a United Kingdom statute). This Act created the present Federal structure by which certain powers were given to the newly-created Commonwealth of Australia. The Constitution established the Commonwealth Parliament and other bodies, and apportioned law-making power between the Commonwealth, on the one hand, and the States, on the other.

Basically, the pattern is that certain specified powers are given to the Commonwealth, for example, defence, interstate and overseas trade and commerce, external affairs, customs and excise. The Commonwealth Parliament has power to make laws only in respect of such matters.

Some of these matters, for instance, customs and excise, are assigned to the Commonwealth Parliament exclusively, so that the State Parliaments can not pass laws on these matters.

The other powers given to the Commonwealth are said to be *concurrent*, meaning that both Commonwealth and State Parliaments have power to legislate. What if the Commonwealth Parliament and State Parliament legislate on the same thing? The Constitution provides that, in the event of inconsistency between State and Commonwealth laws on such a topic, the State Act shall, to the extent of the inconsistency, be invalid. For example, when the Commonwealth Parliament passed the *Family Law Act* 1975, State laws on those aspects of family law covered by the Commonwealth Act became inoperative.

Power to make laws on matters not entrusted to the Commonwealth at all remains exclusively with the States.

4 The Commonwealth Constitution — restrictions on legislative power

Apart from this apportionment of law-making power between Commonwealth and States, the Commonwealth Constitution also contains several restrictions on law-making power, some on the Commonwealth, some on the States, some on both.

For example: s 92 provides unequivocally that interstate trade commerce and intercourse shall be "absolutely free", and thus renders invalid any attempt by State or Commonwealth Parliaments to pass laws which restrict such freedom. Section 116 prevents the Commonwealth from passing a law to establish a religion or to discriminate on the basis of religion. Section 51 (xxxi) provides that the Commonwealth must pay compensation "on just terms" when it compulsorily acquires property.

5 Special legislative procedures

The Commonwealth Constitution remains effective in apportioning and limiting legislative power because it may not be amended by any ordinary Act of the Commonwealth Parliament but only by an Act passed in accordance with s 128. This section requires that any proposed amendment must be put to a referendum and must be accepted by *a majority of the electors* — further, that in *a majority of the States* a majority of the electors must approve. Therefore, for the making of laws to amend the Constitution, we need the participation not only of the Queen, the Senate and the House of Representatives, but of the electors as well.

The Commonwealth Constitution may also prescribe special legislative procedures in other situations, for example, the "deadlock" procedure in s 57. Non-compliance with this procedure led to the High Court ruling invalid the *Petroleum and Mineral Authority Act* 1973.

The State Constitutions can, generally, be amended by the State Parliaments in the same way as any other State statute, but some States have written special amendment procedures into parts of their Constitutions. For example, s 7A of the New South Wales Constitution requires a referendum for any bill to abolish the Upper House, The courts have generally held that such procedures have to be complied with, or the Act will be invalid.

These, then, are the main ways in which legislative power in Australia is limited. The essence of it is the working out of a federal system, which necessarily requires that power be apportioned between the different legislatures in the federation. Such apportionment exists in other federal structures, such as the United States and Canada. It may be useful to summarize the main forms of legal limitation on the law-making powers of the Commonwealth and State Parliaments respectively as follows:

Commonwealth Parliament

(a) The supremacy of the Constitution itself, preserved by the *Statute of Westminster*, s 8, so that it may only be amended by the referendum procedures under s 128.

(b) Territoriality — any law must be for "the peace, order and good government of the Commonwealth" (Constitution, s 51); but the *Statute of Westminster*, s 3, seems to enlarge power.

(c) Specific "heads" of power — any law must be a law "with respect to" one of the matters on which the Parliament is given legislative power under the Constitution, principally in s 51, for example, defence, taxation, etc.

(d) Prohibitions under the Constitution — ss 92, 116, 51 (xxxi), etc.

State Parliaments

(a) Territoriality — any law must be for "the peace, order and good government of" the State (State Constitutions); but the *Australia Act* 1986, s 2 seems to enlarge power.

(b) Exclusive Commonwealth powers — State legislation on matters assigned exclusively to the Commonwealth will be invalid.

(c) Concurrent powers — State legislation will be invalid if it is inconsistent with any Commonwealth legislation on a matter in which legislative power is concurrent (Constitution, s 109).

(d) Prohibitions under the Commonwealth Constitution, for example, s 92.

(e) Any special amendment procedures "entrenched" in the State's own Constitution or other legislation. This limitation is supported by s 6 of the *Australia Act* 1986.

The two major bases for limits on the law-making power of Australian Parliaments have been "the British connection" and the federal arrangement. In Chapter 2 we saw that "the British connection" is no longer a significant factor. What about the limits deriving from the federal arrangement? How can these be changed?

Constitutional Change

Formal amendment of the Commonwealth Constitution is not easy. Experience has shown that it is difficult to obtain the necessary majorities (of electors, and of States) that s 128 requires. To 1988, 40 proposals to amend the Constitution had been put to the electors, but only 8 had been adopted by the necessary majorities. Professor Colin Howard writes: "The Australian constitution is a complicated, rigid, technical and highly misleading document".

One interesting innovation was the establishment of a continuing Australian Constitutional Convention comprising delegates of both government and opposition parties from Federal, State and Territory legislatures, and from local government. The Convention met in 1973 (Sydney), 1975 (Melbourne), 1976 (Hobart), 1978 (Perth) and 1983 (Adelaide) to consider proposals to amend the Constitution. The outcome of the 1974 referendum, when 3 out of 4 proposals were accepted by the electors, was based on prior agreement achieved at the Constitutional Convention.

But it is not always easy to obtain the agreement of the major political parties. The "constitutional crisis" of 1975 raises important questions about the powers of the Senate and of the Governor-General, and agreement has not yet been reached on how to resolve these issues.

There have been other moves towards major constitutional change. Much consciousness-raising work has been done by bodies such as Citizens for Democracy and the Campaign for Constitutional Change which were established in the wake of the events of 1975. A major research project involving a range of experts was established by the Law Foundation of New South Wales in 1981 with the task of stimulating debate on the desirability and possibility of changing the Australian Constitution. The Bicentennial Year, 1988, was suggested as an appropriate focal time for substantial revision of our constitutional arrangements. The centre piece for the Law Foundation project, a book entitled *Australia's Constitution: Time for Change?*, was published in 1983.

Another approach was adopted by Commonwealth Attorney-General Lionel Bowen in bringing to an end the Australian Constitutional Convention when it no longer seemed capable of reaching any significant measure of agreement. Instead he established a Constitutional Commission plus five specialist Advisory Committees consisting, mainly, of people who were not politicians. The Advisory Committees published their reports in 1987 and the Constitutional Commission reported in 1988. A number of proposals for constitutional amendment were recommended, but, following the failure of the four proposals put to the electors in 1988, no further action has been taken.

In 1991, a Constitutional Centenary Conference held in Sydney proposed establishment of a Foundation, headed by Sir Ninian Stephen, to lead a Constitutional Review Process leading to the Centenary of Federation in 2001.

Despite the difficulty of formal amendment, the Constitution today operates in a very different way than it did in 1901.

One factor for change is judicial interpretation. From time to time the High Court of Australia has interpreted the language of the Constitution in ways which enlarge or narrow Commonwealth or State powers, or limitations on those powers.

Another factor is money. The Commonwealth Government has gained control of the major sources of revenue (especially customs and excise duties and income tax). In redistributing some of this revenue to the State Governments under s 96, it is able to require the States to implement Commonwealth Government policies even in areas where the Commonwealth Parliament itself has no power to make laws, for example, housing, roads, hospitals, universities.

A third factor for change has been through Federal-State cooperation in a variety of forms. The Constitution itself provides in s 51 (xxxvii) for State Parliaments to refer powers to the Commonwealth Parliament, and one proposal for amending the Constitution is to allow a broader interchange of powers. Section 51 (xxxviii) provides for joint Commonwealth-State legislative activity to deal with matters which neither side could have dealt with in 1901; this power was first used in 1980 in resolving a number of issues concerning authority over off-shore areas. It was used again in the process of ending United Kingdom authority by enactment of the *Australia Acts* in 1986. Federal-State co-operation also occurs at the executive level through a variety of consultative and other bodies.

So the Commonwealth Constitution has evolved, and continues to evolve, despite the difficulties in securing formal amendments. The major movement in this evolution is towards centralization. As Professor Colin Howard writes (in *The Constitution, Power and Politics*): "... throughout the whole of the short history of the Australian Federation the states have steadily declined in independence and responsibility in relation to the Commonwealth. There has been an uninterrupted and continuing shift of effective political power to the centre".

7
Courts and the Interpretation of Legislation

Legislation is the most obvious source of law, and in many ways the most important. We think of the formal *creation* of law as being a matter for Parliament (or its delegates in the case of delegated legislation), while the proper function of the courts is the *application* of those laws to the facts of a particular case. Parliament decides what the law is; the courts apply the law to the facts of particular cases. This neat division of functions is often a fair description of what the courts and Parliament do. In most cases of murder, as in most cases of traffic offences, the problems are entirely factual. Was it the accused who fired the shot that killed the victim? Did the defendant park in the limited zone for over the permitted time? There is no *legal* problem in such cases; once the facts are established, it will be quite clear whether the offence has been committed or not.

However, there are many cases in which this description does not work at all. Often the court has an important part to play in deciding *what the statute means* (a legal question) not merely *what has happened* (a factual question). This may seem surprising. After all, statutes are enacted in English, and they are usually drafted with great care and then debated in Parliament. It may not be immediately apparent why they should be hard to understand, certainly for judges who are trained lawyers and should be able to work out even complicated provisions. So, let us first illustrate the kind of problem that can arise.

Litterbugs, Mark 1

A State Parliament passes a statute including the provision:

> Any person who throws litter in the street shall be liable to a fine not exceeding fifty dollars.

Where defendants plead Not Guilty, the only question, usually, will be the factual one; did they do what they are alleged to have done? If the court holds that they did, they will be convicted and probably punished; if not, of course they will be acquitted. The only difficulties the court will face will be in deciding the facts: for example, it may have to decide which of two witnesses is telling the truth. If it finds the charge proved it will then have to decide what penalty to impose on the defendant.

However, one day a problem case may come up. Three law students, returning from a picnic, are charged with the offence. They cheerfully admit the facts, but . . .

Andrew says that he did in fact throw litter, but not *in the street* — he threw various bits of paper on the pavement, in a park, and in a shop doorway, but this is not throwing litter in the street.

Marjorie admits that she left litter in the street, but then goes on to deny that she *threw* it — it dropped out of her hands accidentally, and the word "throw" only applies to people who *intend* to place litter in the street.

Paul argues that what he left in the street was not *litter*, in the sense of something useless which is abandoned, but that it was a useful article, namely the evening newspaper, which he left on a seat in a bus shelter for anyone who wanted to read it. (Paul, beginning to enjoy himself, was going on to argue that leaving the paper in the bus shelter was not leaving it "in the street", but, after a glance at the expression on the magistrate's face, decided he had said enough.)

Thus, even a simple section like this can lead to a number of arguments about its meaning and scope. The students, rather than denying the facts, argued that what they did fell outside the scope of the section and was therefore not criminal. When the court rules on such arguments it is said to be "interpreting" the legislation. By interpretation, the court can determine the scope of the section. For example, if the court held that "throw" only applied to deliberate acts, it would be restricting the scope of the section by taking a narrow interpretation. If it held that the word covered accidental or careless acts as well, it would be extending the scope of the section by a broad interpretation.

Litterbugs, Mark 2

In fact, most laws are expressed in a wordier form than this (statutes and regulations make notoriously heavy reading, but insomniacs sometimes find them useful). The reason is not that lawyers get paid by the word, but that people drafting statutes try to make as clear as possible the situations to which the law applies. Having examined some of the problems in applying our original simple "litterbug" provision, it is easier to see the thinking behind the sort of phrasing you might find in real legislation, for instance:

> Any person who throws, drops or leaves any litter, waste or other matter in any street, park or public place...

Do you agree that this makes it clearer whether the law applies in the situations we described earlier? The rephrasing of the provision made it longer and less elegant, but perhaps made its application clearer.

It is obviously desirable that the application of the law should be clear. In provisions that make certain behaviour a crime, in particular, the legislator should make clear what behaviour is forbidden. Suppose instead of our "litterbug" provision the legislation merely said: "Anyone who misbehaves in the park commits an offence". In one sense, that provision is clear and simple. But in another, it is not: it fails to indicate to the users of the park what sort of behaviour is prohibited, since it is very much a matter of opinion what counts as "misbehaviour". So there is a constant pressure on legislators to spell out what they mean so that the application of the law is as certain as possible. When they try to do so, the result is often rather long and convoluted sentences.

But the elaborate phrasing of legislation often brings problems of its own. Long, complex sentences can sometimes be interpreted in different ways. Perhaps more important, even when several words are used instead of one there is still room for uncertainty. Take our re-written "litterbug" provision. Is a schoolyard a "public place"? If it is, does a teacher who throws a ball to a child in the course of a game commit an offence? Surely not, and yet look at the words: "Any person who throws ... any ... matter in any ... public place ...". It seems absurd if the teacher has committed a crime, but how can we avoid that conclusion? How would you argue the case, if you were representing the teacher who was prosecuted for the offence? How would you decide, if you were the judge?

We have tried to show why the language of legislation is often complex, and also that even with very carefully written legislation, courts have to resolve tricky questions in applying the law. "Interpretation" of legislation is a significant part of the everyday work of courts. How do they do it? How can we know what meaning they are going to choose? The answer to the second question is that very often we do not; in fact the presence of the case in court usually means that at least one lawyer thinks that there is something to be said for each side. We can say something, though, about the way the courts approach the task.

The Legislature's "Intention"

The fundamental principle usually stated by the judges is that they must simply work out what Parliament *intended* in enacting the statute. They must then apply the statute in accordance with Parliament's intention.

But the real problem is how to find out what Parliament did intend. It is hardly feasible for the judge to adjourn proceedings while he or she troops off down to Parliament House to ask the assembled legislators what they had in mind.

Even if this were feasible, it would not be very helpful. The judge might want to know whether they intended, by the use of the word "throw", to penalize accidental dropping of litter. Some of the Members of Parliament might have intended the word "throw" to have this wider operation, others might have intended it to cover only deliberate acts, and most of them probably had not even thought of the problem at all. Some may have been resting their eyelids during the parliamentary debate. Further, the Parliament which enacted it will probably not consist of the same people as make up the present Parliament.

A possible solution is to refer to the debates in Parliament about the legislation. Parliamentary proceedings are all written down word for word and published in official reports known as Hansard. Those debates might give a good indication of what was intended (if we charitably overlook the abuse, incoherence and irrelevancies that fill many pages of Hansard). Curiously, our legal system, unlike some others, has traditionally avoided this apparently obvious line of inquiry. The reasons have been that the legislation itself is the formal and final expression of Parliament's intention, and recourse to debates leading up to the legislation might be confusing: it is better, the argument goes, for the courts to base their decision only on the wording of the legislation itself. Another argument in favour of the traditional approach is that once you start looking behind the legislation, it is hard to know where to stop. If we can refer to Parliamentary debates, why not also to party policies, or speeches by the relevant politicians outside Parliament, or reports of inquiries, law reform commissions and others that led to the legislation? Referring to all these things, however, would mean that court cases would never end, and the already high costs of litigation would skyrocket. Either it is all relevant, or none of it is, concludes the traditionalist, with a triumphant glare.

Despite such arguments, the courts' attitude is softening to some extent, and in more recent cases courts sometimes do refer to some Parliamentary speeches, and such things as law reform commission reports, to help them understand, if not the language of the Act, at least the problem that it was addressing. Legislation has been passed encouraging courts to do this, at least in cases where the meaning of the relevant provision of the Act is unclear. But it remains true that the primary focus is on the words of the legislation itself, and the courts mainly look to these words in their search for the "intention" of the legislature.

The trouble is, as we have seen, that this doesn't always work. The fact is that the courts have to apply general words to particular fact situations, and there is often a genuine doubt about what they mean. The problem of finding a meaning is not much helped by talking about the legislature's "intention", if you end up staring at the same words. The "intention of the legislature" is really a legal fiction. Yet one way or another courts have to produce a result: how can they do it?

Courts' Approaches to the Interpretation of Statutes

Judges themselves have often tried to explain their approach. They have sometimes spoken as if there were rules that governed the process. One of these is known as the "literal rule" of statutory interpretation: words are to be read in their ordinary and natural meaning, and then mechanically applied to the facts. The court's job, based on this view, is not to think about whether the results are fair or reasonable or not, it is only to *apply* the statute to the facts. Whatever the result, it must have been the "intention" of Parliament. (If Parliament does not like the results, it can change the law by amending the statute.)

The "literal rule" is, of course, nonsense. The reason why the point is being argued is that the words are not clear; there is a real doubt about what they mean. It is no solution to claim, as the literal rule does, "The words mean what they say".

Although it is nonsense, the literal rule has a certain appeal. First, it allows the judges to avoid personal responsibility for their decisions. They can say: "It is the statute that is producing this result, not me. I really had nothing to do with it". That is a natural human reaction when confronted with a difficult choice, and some judges, like other people, prefer to take the easy way out.

There is another reason for the persistence of the literal rule. English political thought has long been much influenced by the idea of the classification of powers in a State as judicial, executive or legislative, and the undesirability of having the same body exercise more than one kind of power. If judges can persuade themselves that they are only *applying* the legislation, then they are sticking to their type of power, the judicial. But if they freely acknowledge that they have a choice in the matter, then they are, in a sense, sharing legislative power with the Parliament. This is inconsistent with the idea of separation of powers, and it is a function which many judges were, and some old-fashioned ones still are, reluctant to admit.

The "literal rule" is less a rule than a way of approaching the task of statutory interpretation. Another approach is represented by the "golden rule", which qualifies the literal rule by saying that the court will not follow the literal meaning of the words if they do not embody the legislature's intention or if they lead to an "absurdity". This does not help much, because we can only look at the words to discover the (fictional) "intention" of the legislature, and the literalist will say that you have to read the statute as a *whole*, a process which often leads to the same conclusion as the golden rule. And, of course, what is absurd to one judge may look quite sensible to another.

Yet another approach is represented by the "mischief rule" under which judges may consider what mischief (or problem) the statute was intended to remedy so that they may interpret it in order to achieve that result. This "mischief" rule stands in contrast to the "literal" rule and is akin to what is sometimes called the "purposive" approach to statutory interpretation. Increasingly judges are being encouraged to adopt such an approach.

These differences of approach can have important consequences. Take as an example the interpretation of federal taxation legislation. In a number of cases in the 1970s the High Court upheld appeals against tax liability by wealthy taxpayers on the basis of a "literal" interpretation of the statute. In the early 1980s the High Court moved away from this approach, assisted by a new section added in 1981 to the federal *Acts Interpretation Act*. Section 15AA requires courts to prefer an interpretation of federal Acts "that would promote the purpose or object underlying the Act" rather than one which would not, and parliamentary draftspersons are now beginning to spell out in statutes the underlying purpose or object. The result of this more purposive approach was to make it more difficult for people to avoid tax by creating artificial schemes.

There are a great many "rules" of statutory interpretation, and whole books have been written on the subject. These rules are of different kinds. Some present no problem. For example, we have already referred to the rule that in interpreting a statute a court is not allowed to use Parliamentary reports. This rule may be a good one or a bad one, but it is quite clear and intelligible. So, too, is the rule that a statute must be read as a whole.

Other rules designed to help judges interpret legislation, particularly those described as "presumptions", are rather curious. Many of these are in Latin, which may account for their dwindling popularity. For example, *generalia specialibus non derogant* (general words do not prevail over specific ones), *expressio unius est exclusio alterius* (expressing one thing excludes the other). These are often like proverbs in that they can be quoted to support any conclusion whatever; for example, if I quote, "Every word and clause must be given some effect", you can retort with equal authority: "Ah, but if words are inadvertently inserted, or if they are repugnant to the rest of the statute, they may be rejected as surplusage". One legal scholar put it nicely when he said that these presumptions "hunt in pairs". (So, of course, do non-legal proverbs: contrast "Look before you leap" with "He who hesitates is lost".)

However, there are some presumptions which do reflect prevailing attitudes of the courts. An example is the presumption that Parliament did not intend to widen the criminal law beyond the clear words of the statute, so that any lack of clarity in a criminal statute is likely to be resolved in favour of the defendant. It is still true, though, that even this presumption may have to compete against others, such as the mischief rule.

Some of these rules and presumptions have a history; they crystallize the attitudes of judges in various formative periods of the law. Even today, it would be going too far to say that they are all meaningless. Taken together, they do indicate a characteristically "legal" approach to interpretation. They can sometimes be useful, providing they are not taken at face value: it is not possible to remove all uncertainties in legislation by a set of "rules" of interpretation. Statutory interpretation, just like the interpretation of precedents, requires the court to make a creative decision, and this decision may well be a difficult one, requiring judgment in resolving difficult policy considerations. Judges have to do this, whether they like it or not, and they do not help matters by doing it behind a smoke-screen of rules and presumptions.

Vehicles in the Park

A further illustration may clarify this.* Suppose a notice reads, "No vehicles allowed in the park". Clearly that prohibits motor cars: clearly it does not prohibit roller skates. A motor car is obviously a vehicle; a pair of wheeled shoes is not. But suppose a court has to decide whether the notice prohibits a child's battery powered toy motor car. Is that a "vehicle"? In deciding such a case, a court might (and, we suggest should) consider the policy issues involved. Vehicles are prohibited because a park is a place for beauty, quiet and recreation, not a thoroughfare. However, this child's toy is an instrument of recreation, not transport, and its use is not likely to pollute the park or unduly disturb the other park users. Parks are, among other things, for children to play in, and there is no very good reason to stop them playing with electric toy cars.

If a court took this view, it would hold that "vehicle" did not include electric toy cars and they are therefore allowed in the park. On the other hand, a court might say that even a toy car disturbs the peace of a park, and the prohibition is intended to preserve the peace against even toy cars. Such a court would hold that the toy car was a "vehicle", and thus not permitted in the park.

Our point is this: a court should not avoid the task of having to decide for itself the purposes and policies behind legislation. In deciding this case, it should discuss the sort of arguments we have set out. In particular, a court should not fall back on formulas, and say, for example: "We hold that this car is a 'vehicle' because the local council intended to exclude such cars". That is no reason at all.

Selling Liquor to Drunks

We may illustrate this further by looking at a case decided in 1884. A licensed publican was convicted of the offence of selling liquor to a drunken person. His defence was that he did not know the man was drunk. The question of interpretation was whether the statute caught all publicans who supplied liquor to drunks, or only those who did so *knowingly*. The court held the former interpretation was correct, and the conviction was upheld: the offence was committed even if the accused did not know the man was drunk. The judge gave these reasons for the decision: firstly, *other* sections of the Act contained the word "knowingly" in the definition of offences, and the omission of that word from this offence suggested that knowledge was not necessary for a conviction. Secondly, the judge discussed "the

---

* This illustration is stolen from *The Concept of Law* by Professor Herbert Hart. Both this chapter and Chapter 13 draw heavily on Professor Hart's writings, some of which are mentioned in the list of suggested reading at the end of this book.

general scope of the Act, which is for the repression of drunkenness" and said:

> I believe the reason for making this prohibition absolute was that there must be a great temptation to a publican to sell liquor without regard to the sobriety of the customer, and it was thought right to put upon the publican the responsibility of determining whether his customer is sober.

The judge thought that these considerations outweighed the general principle that nobody can be guilty of a crime unless he or she has a "guilty mind". Some lawyers disagree with the decision, and argue that since there was a doubt in the meaning of the Act, it should have been resolved in favour of the accused. But the case, whether right or wrong, does bring out the point that in interpreting Acts the court is doing more than juggling with words; it is deciding questions of policy, just as Parliament has to when it makes the Acts in the first place.

Interpreting the Constitution

In the examples discussed above, the courts were interpreting a statute for the purpose of deciding whether a person was guilty of an offence. Of course, it is often necessary to interpret statutes for other purposes too; a court might have to decide if a person can claim a tax deduction, or whether a public official has a certain power, or whether delegated legislation is authorized by the Act under which it was passed.

One of the statutes the courts have to interpret is the Commonwealth Constitution itself. This is such an important statute that decisions on its meaning are central to the whole legal system. This is particularly so as constitutional provisions are often necessarily general, and there is a great deal of room for the courts to interpret them in accordance with the changing times. For example, s 92 of the Australian Constitution provides that "trade, commerce and intercourse between the States shall be absolutely free". There is a long line of cases on the meaning of this section, reflecting not only new and unexpected factual situations, but changing conceptions on the part of the High Court about the proper relationship between the Commonwealth and the States. These interpretations can involve quite important changes of direction, as in the 1988 case *Cole v Whitfield*, where the High Court adopted a complete rethinking of the purpose and scope of the section.

Interpreting the Constitution may have one consequence that is not the result of interpreting any other form of legislation: a court may strike down a statute (that is, declare it invalid) because it considers it is not consistent with the constitutional provisions. If that happens — and it sometimes does — the statute is deprived of legal effect.

Further, it may not be open to Commonwealth Parliament to overcome the court's decision by passing a new Act without the Constitution itself being amended. For example, in one case some years ago the Commonwealth Parliament passed an Act about radio broadcasting. It claimed to have the power to do so under s 51(v) of the Constitution which gives the Commonwealth Parliament power to pass laws with respect to "postal, telegraphic, telephonic or other like services". The whole case turned on the question whether these words, enacted in 1901, covered radio broadcasting or not. The High Court decided that they did, and the legislation was therefore valid. But if the court had interpreted the words of s 51(v) as not including radio broadcasting (or television), then it would not have been open to Parliament to have overcome this interpretation by an amending Act.

Again, when the courts decided that the Commonwealth's defence power did not authorize the enactment of the *Communist Party Dissolution Act* 1950, all that the Government could do was to seek to have the Constitution altered so as clearly to confer such a power. However, the bill did not get the votes of enough of the electors at the referendum to alter the Constitution, so the last word on the interpretation of the Constitution remained with the courts.

The powers of a court to invalidate statutes are very much increased if a constitution contains "Bills of Rights" clauses. These may involve such general standards as "freedom of speech" and "due process of law"; and the court can declare invalid any legislation or decision which it finds is contrary to those standards. Clearly this is a great power, for such phrases are so general and vague in themselves that the judges must play a very large part in deciding just what they mean. In the United States, for example, the Supreme Court has used such standards in creating a great deal of the law relating to the question of race relations between white and black Americans. Such decisions impinge considerably on political questions, and the political views of the judges in such countries are much more fully discussed and debated than they are in a country like Australia, which has no Bill of Rights.

Although the constitutional decisions of our own High Court are important and may have important political repercussions, they rarely involve the Court in the kind of directly "political" decisions made by the Supreme Court of the United States, or by courts of other countries whose Constitutions have a Bill of Rights. If Australia does adopt a Bill of Rights (this is discussed in Chapter 12) then we might expect a significant change in the role of the High Court, and a new interest in the decisions and attitudes of its judges.

The same problems of interpretation arise in regard to delegated legislation, regulations and the like as with statutes, and are handled by the courts in a similar fashion. But it should be stressed that, in most instances, legislation is clear enough to cover the main situations with which Parliament is concerned. It is only on the fringes, so to speak, in marginal situations, that questions of interpretation will come before the courts.

The main point to be noted is this: although Parliament (or its delegates) is our primary source of law today, the role of the courts can be most important. The courts do not *make* legislation but they can be highly influential, firstly, in deciding whether the Parliament itself (or its delegate) had *power* to make it, and secondly, in deciding what is the *meaning and scope* of the legislation which it has made. In interpreting legislation, the courts can be regarded as partners in the legislative process.

Statutory Interpretation and Case Law

We have seen that law is created by both legislation and judicial decisions. When the judicial decisions interpret legislation, the two forms of law-making work together. A case interpreting a statute is just as much a precedent as any other judicial decision. Thus the case in 1884 about the publican is an authoritative precedent in England that a publican who supplies liquor to a drunk person is guilty of an offence even if he or she does not know the person is drunk. A later English judge will be bound by that decision unless sitting in a higher court (say the Court of Appeal or the House of Lords), in which case the judge can overrule it. That is, the doctrine of precedent applies to cases on the meaning of statutes as much as to any other type of case.

Quite a body of law has grown up around some statutes, and some words have become encrusted with a series of cases explaining what they mean. Sometimes there are cases which decide the meaning of a word like "malice". Sometimes a word or a phrase which has been interpreted in one statute is used again in a later statute, and the courts will often follow the earlier interpretations of the word in the new legislation.

Interpretation Generally

Courts spend a lot of their time explaining what words mean. All sorts of documents have to be "interpreted" as well as statutes. Wills, contracts, deeds, and other documents often give rise to problems of meaning which come to the courts for resolution. In commercial matters, where a great many documents are of standard form, phrases are used which have been interpreted in many previous cases, and which the parties trust will be interpreted the same way in their case. Courts are reluctant to change their minds about the meaning of words in this area because the people concerned may have used the words intending them to have the effect given to them in previous decisions. In that case a new interpretation would give to the document a meaning which the parties did not intend it to have. This partly explains why the law contains so many old and peculiar phrases. It does not however *justify* the use of unduly convoluted or technical language in legislation. Citizens should be able to read and understand legislation, even if this takes some effort in relation to complex topics. In recent years there has been a welcome move towards "plain English" legislation, and it has led to considerable improvement in the writing of statutes and other legal documents.

Bishop Hoadley once said: "Nay whoever hath an absolute authority to interpret any written or spoken laws it is he who is the lawgiver to all intents and purposes and not the person who first wrote or spake them". On this extreme view there is no certainty at all: any document that comes before the court, whether it is a will, a contract or a statute, means just what the court says it means, which could be anything. And indeed, there are some cases which seem to interpret documents or statutes in a way which would have startled the people who drew up the original documents or statutes.

This is nevertheless an exaggerated view, which considerably distorts the operation of the legal system. We have already pointed out the creative choices that have to be made in the course of interpreting legislation. In the past judges were reluctant to acknowledge explicitly the degree of choice — and therefore power — that they really had. But it is possible to go too far in stressing the point, and to obscure the important limitations on judicial inventiveness.

The system of enactment of general rules by Parliament and their subsequent application and modification in judicial decisions reflects a compromise. The compromise is between the need for certainty (which would be promoted by the minimum need for interpretation by the courts) and the need to leave open many of the details of the rules which can only be intelligently worked out when they arise in a concrete case (which would be promoted by vague, general rules). It is easy, and proper, to frame such a general rule as: "Whoever owns a thing is entitled to possess it". It is necessary, though, to have an indeterminate "unless . . . " at the end. Otherwise how would the law handle the situation of the lunatic who started shooting up people with his pistol? We need to have a rule allowing us to take the pistol from him. It is necessary to cater for exceptions; it is futile to try to predict them all in advance.

One way of expressing the balance between certainty and flexibility inherent in legal rules is to think of them as having a solid core but fuzzy edges. The solid core represents the easy, straightforward cases where the rule is clearly applicable; the fuzzy edges represent the difficult, uncertain cases, where a creative choice is required. To say that courts merely apply the law ignores the fuzzy edges. To say that courts can declare the law to be anything they like ignores the solid core.

8

Lawyers

The word "lawyers" usually refers to practising members of the legal profession: barristers and solicitors. As we shall see, the legal profession in Australia is organised on a State or Territory basis, and there are some differences among the States, although the general pattern and historical tradition is based on the way the profession is organized in England.

We use the word "lawyers" also in a wider sense, to include certain other people who are legally qualified, or otherwise closely associated with the law, but are not practising barristers or solicitors. We start with the most obvious category, judges.

Judges

Who appoints judges? Formally, the Governors of the States, and the Governor-General in the case of the High Court and other federal courts. In practice, because the Governors and Governor-Generals follow the advice they receive from the government, it is the government of the day that makes the appointments. Does this mean that judicial appointments are political? In some ways, yes. Especially in the case of the High Court, governments naturally tend to appoint people whose decisions they think will be in line with that government's policies (though people do not always perform as expected when appointed to the bench). Also, a judicial appointment can have political overtones, including gratitude for past political service to a party, or even the desire to move an awkward politician out of the way. Several former Commonwealth Attorneys-General, from both sides of politics, have been appointed to the High Court of Australia. These factors should not be overstated, though. Most judicial decisions have nothing to do with government policy; even the High Court is much more limited in what it can do about government policies than, say, the United States Supreme Court. Another limiting factor is that in practice, especially in the case of the higher courts, judges are generally chosen from among a small number of senior practitioners regarded by the legal profession as acceptable for appointment. There is considerable consultation between the Attorney-General (Commonwealth or State, depending on which court is involved) and the leaders of the legal profession, such as the President of the Law Council of Australia or of the Bar Association of the relevant State or Territory. It seems that this process tends to produce the most "successful" barristers. In this context, a "successful" barrister is probably one who practices in "mainstream" (feminist lawyers might say "malestream") areas such as commercial law and equity; who is well-known and respected by other lawyers; and who is able to attract a lot of work despite charging high fees. When barristers are appointed to the bench, it is not uncommon for congratulatory speeches by leaders of the profession to refer to the new judge's previous "busy and lucrative practice".

The high incomes of the top lawyers, however, can create a problem. Appointment to the bench of a higher court is in one sense the ultimate career achievement of a practising lawyer. But in recent times the incomes of the more successful practitioners have risen much faster than judicial salaries, so that, even allowing for pensions and other advantages, appointment as a judge may mean a considerable drob in salary. This has apparently led to some difficulty — it varies according to the court — in attracting the most successful practitioners to the bench.

The pool of lawyers from which judges are selected does not represent the community in such matters as gender, class, race or education. Women constituted only 17.2% of lawyers in 1986, the number having grown from 0.2% in 1911 and 6% in 1971. Within the profession, women tend to have lower incomes than men. They tend to work in areas such as family law rather than more lucrative areas such as commercial law, and they tend to be employed solicitors rather than partners, or barristers. Members of minority groups are under-represented among lawyers. Law has traditionally been dominated by people in the higher socio-economic groups, and this continues. As with women, those lawyers who do come from minority groups, or lower socio-economic groups, tend to be concentrated in the less "successful" and lucrative levels of the profession. The net result is that lawyers constitute, as David Weisbrot says in his book *Australian Lawyers* (on which much of this information is based), "an elite profession". The causes of this are many and varied. They include, for example, the very high entry standards of Law in the universities, where most lawyers these days obtain their academic qualifications — and as is well known, academic success at school is linked with advantages of birth.

Especially in the higher courts, judges are mainly drawn from among the most senior and eminent barristers, and the elite background of lawyers in general is accentuated in the pattern of appointment to the bench.

Nearly all judges are men. There have been only two women ever appointed to a State Supreme Court, and one woman appointed to the High Court. In the Family Court of Australia there are a significant number of women, and the first Chief Judge was a woman (the second is a man); but even in this court, in 1992 only 7 of the 55 judges were women.

A study of the High Court found that "the typical High Court Justice is a male white Protestant... of British ethnic origins. He is from upper middle rather than upper class background". A similar picture emerges for other courts. In Victoria 20 out of 21 judges had attended private schools, and only one lived in a Labor electorate. In New South Wales about a third had fathers who were lawyers, and another third had fathers who were in business or the professions. Two-thirds had attended private schools, and most of the rest had gone to elite State schools.

Some commentators have taken the view that this experience, as well as other factors, makes judges conservative. Roger Douglas wrote: "Law breeds conservatism; the greater the lawyer, the more likely it is that he will be, even though no active politician, a 'sound man' from the point of view of a non-Labor Government". Stan Ross wrote that judges are members of the establishment: "the law does not often attract those with a crusading or rebellious spirit". And David Weisbrot: "the social background of lawyers and judges means that there is an inevitable infusion of upper-middle class values into the legal system and legal ideology". By contrast, the NSW Law Society probably expressed the official view of the profession when it said that "the socio-economic background of members of the profession does not affect the ability of the legal profession to render legal services for all sectors of the community and does not make the profession unsympathetic to the needs of the disadvantaged sectors".

What do you think? For our part, we agree with the following statement of Australian law deans, which is particularly applicable to judges:

> Law affects all members of the community irrespective of wealth, ethnic background, gender or any other social or individual difference. If the law is to respond to the needs of these different groups, lawyers themselves need to reflect the broadest possible social mix.

The only formal requirement for judicial appointment is a specified period of legal practice. Judges take up their appointments immediately, without any special training. There are, of course, different approaches. In many European systems there is a particular course of training and career path for judges. In the United States, some judges are elected periodically. The common law tradition seems based on the assumption that judges' prior experience as advocates will equip them to decide cases wisely. Whether this is so, and whether the community is best served by the selection of judges from the sort of people described, are intriguing questions.

Whoever they are, and however they were appointed, judges are supposed to be totally independent, and to act "without fear or favour". This idea is regarded as a fundamental part of our legal system, and is the basis of some aspects of judges' tenure of office. Independence of the judges from the Crown was won for the judges by Parliament in the *Act of Settlement*, 1701. This Act provided that judges should hold office not, as previously, "at the King's pleasure", but "during good behaviour": judges could be removed from office by the Crown only after a request from each House of Parliament. And to prevent the Crown from imposing financial pressures on judges, the Act provided that their salaries should be fixed and should not be reduced during their terms of office.

This solution has provided the basis for judicial independence in many countries. Similar provisions are found in the laws of the Australian Commonwealth and States, though life tenure is nowadays replaced by provisions that judges should hold office until a fixed retiring age, usually 70.

In addition judges are immune from legal liability in respect of anything they say or do in the course of judicial proceedings. By these rules, it is hoped, the courts will be independent and impartial so that judges can decide cases without any fear of displeasing either the Government or anyone else.

But of course these protections do not guarantee that judges will be honest, impartial and unafraid. They cannot prevent a judge taking a bribe, or acting from personal bias or prejudice, or from fear of someone who threatens to blow up his or her house and family. The only real guarantee is the quality of the people who become judges; and this in turn depends largely on the standards of the profession from which they are drawn.

Scandals about judges have been mercifully few in Australian history. However, the 1980s saw some events that gave rise to a measure of anxiety about the functioning of the courts and the conduct of judges. In New South Wales, a former Chief Stipendiary Magistrate was convicted and imprisoned for attempting to pervert the course of justice. A District Court judge was tried and acquitted of the same offence. The most publicised event, however, was a series of parliamentary inquiries and court proceedings in 1985 and 1986 concerning the late Mr Justice Lionel Murphy of the High Court. Justice Murphy had been a reforming Attorney-General in the Whitlam government in the 1970s, and his judgments on the High Court were often innovative in both style and content. Controversy raged on the propriety or otherwise of what he was said to have done, and on whether the proceedings against him were justifiable. He was tried and convicted, but his appeal succeeded on the ground that the trial judge had misdirected the jury. On his retrial, he was acquitted by a jury. Parliamentary inquiries examining the question whether he should be removed from the High Court were abandoned when it was learned that he was gravely ill. He died in October 1986.

In response to these incidents, the New South Wales government passed controversial legislation establishing a Judicial Commission to deal with complaints against judges. Also in New South Wales, five magistrates were effectively removed when the legislation establishing their courts was repealed and re-enacted in another form. They succeeded in setting aside the decision not to re-appoint them on the ground that they had not been given "natural justice", a matter discussed in Chapter 12. Such events, and the public controversies that surround them, have meant that questions of judicial conduct and security of tenure are much more prominent than they were. It is difficult to say, however, whether the higher profile of these issues reflects lower standards of behaviour than in earlier times. Gossip has it that in the past some judges may have been put under some pressure to resign, and did so rather than face public accusations.

Such matters are deeply troubling. But it is easy to overgeneralise from particular cases. Our own opinion is that courts in Australia in the vast majority of cases deal with cases honestly and diligently, and that gross incompetence or improper behaviour is very rare among judges and magistrates. We still think it is true to say, as we did in earlier editions, that we have much to be grateful for, and a high tradition to preserve.

Magistrates

Australian States adopted the ancient English practice of entrusting minor judicial work and associated functions to lay persons as unpaid "Justices of the Peace". Justices of the Peace need no special qualifications, and they are appointed by the Governor "during pleasure only" which means that they may be dismissed at any time.

In Australia, as in England, this tradition is giving way to the demands of a more complex society, and the judicial functions of the Justices have been transferred to paid, professionally trained magistrates, especially in the more populous parts of the country. These magistrates were formerly appointed from the ranks of the public service, not from the practising profession. Nowadays, however, legal qualifications are increasingly required. They are appointed by the Governor on the advice of the Public Service Board or Commissioner. In the past they have had less security of tenure and protection than judges and were subject to the same kind of discipline as other public servants. James Crawford in his authoritative book *Australian Courts of Law* relates how in South Australia magistrates were placed in the same government department as Crown prosecutors. The Supreme Court held that they could not deal with criminal cases, on the grounds of bias, one of the aspects of "natural justice" discussed in Chapter 12. Today, in all States except Queensland, magistrates hold office under separate legislation, with security of tenure.

Magistrates and Justices of the Peace exercise jurisdiction over a wide variety of criminal offences, though generally the less serious ones. They also deal with cases involving small debts, tenancy matters, children's cases, and some other civil matters. Their work is regarded as "minor" by many lawyers used to the more glamorous superior courts and large amounts of money, and magistrates occupy a fairly lowly place in the legal fraternity. But to those who come before them, often poor, bewildered and without legal assistance, their work is not minor and their powers are not small.

Other Lawyers

Some lawyers are employed in the service of the Crown. The *Attorney-General* (at both State and Federal levels) is legal adviser to the Crown and ranks first in precedence among members of the Bar. The office is held by an elected member of Parliament who is, thereby, a Minister of the Crown. He or she does not engage in private practice but has a number of important public functions in relation to such matters as criminal prosecutions, and the protection of public rights. The office of *Solicitor-General* in Australia (unlike its counterpart in England) is non-political: the Solicitor-General is the principal adviser to the Attorney-General and gives the government legal advice on important matters.

Crown Prosecutors are barristers in the service of the Crown whose responsibility is the prosecution of indictable criminal offences, that is, those more serious offences tried by judge and jury. *Crown Solicitors* are permanent public servants who act as legal advisers to the government. *Parliamentary counsel* are responsible for drafting of bills and other documents. In the 1980s, the office of *Director of Public Prosecutions* (the New South Wales title varies slightly) was established by the Commonwealth and the States of Victoria and Queensland, to take responsibility for most government prosecutions. There is an advantage in having decisions about the prosecution of major cases (especially sensitive ones, such as the prosecution of a politician) made by an independent officer, rather than being the responsibility of the Attorney-General, an elected politician. Other legal officers do legal work for particular departments, administer legal aid systems, and carry out other public functions.

Some lawyers do not "practise" law, but go into other fields such as politics or government service or business where their legal training can often be useful. Other lawyers, although they practise as such, work exclusively for one client, usually a big company or group of companies, and have their offices in the company's building. Many of these lawyers, and those in some firms of solicitors which specialize in company work, find themselves doing work which is more like general business advice than the practice of law as it is commonly understood. Some lawyers go to work in international organizations. Some unusually foolish ones become "academic" lawyers and spend their time teaching at law schools and writing books like this.

It is a mistake to think that "doing law" only means becoming a solicitor or barrister.

Solicitors

Solicitors work in offices, and spend their days on the telephone, interviewing clients, dictating letters to their secretaries, drawing up documents like wills and mortgages, and preparing cases for hearing. They do appear in courts and argue cases, but not often, and usually only in the lower courts. They sometimes practise on their own, but more often set up firms, or "partnerships", which range in size from two or three to much larger partnerships. In recent times, particularly in the 1980s, these firms have tended to become larger, as a result of numerous mergers of already large firms, resulting in some firms having over a hundred solicitors, and having branches in several Australian States and Territories. Some of these firms also have associations with firms in other countries, or establish their own overseas offices. Each firm has an office (and sometimes a branch office too) with secretaries, computers, books, and lots of files. The solicitors in a firm usually form a hierarchy of seniority: there may be senior partners, junior partners, associates, and lowly "employed solicitors"; most lowly of all are the articled clerks.

Solicitors participate in all kinds of legal work; as we shall see, they differ from barristers in the way they participate. Many firms concentrate on wills and probate, conveyancing (property transactions), tax advice, and other non-litigious work (that is, work that does not involve a court case), while others do a lot of court work, whether motor car accident cases, industrial accidents, workers' compensation, tenancy cases or company work. There is specialization within firms as well as between them; most substantial firms have their conveyancing expert, their litigation expert, and so on. You can usually tell which is which; the conveyancer is always on the phone or asking you to sign something, the litigation expert is either in court, or rushing around looking for a missing witness. Solicitors keep office hours from nine to five, though some work longer, and between those hours they are usually very busy. In terms of documents being signed, people telling other people what to do, arrangements being made, the phone ringing, people coming in for appointments, a great deal *happens* in solicitors' offices.

Solicitors often have close and lasting relationships with many of their clients. You may go to a solicitor about a motor car accident, and if you are satisfied with the service, you may have the solicitor draw up your will, do legal work when you buy a new house, and advise you on tax. You might make the solicitor the executor of your will, and after your death your children might refer all their work to the solicitor — thus many solicitors act in a variety of matters for an individual, and sometimes become the solicitor for a whole family. This is why solicitors' firms usually keep their original names even after the original partners have died; by that time the firm has accumulated a number of regular clients who will stick to the firm even if there are changes in personnel. It also explains why a "practice" can become very valuable, and a successful practitioner can often sell his or her share in the practice for a considerable sum on retirement. Solicitors becoming partners in a firm often have to pay the firm to let them become partners, since a partnership in a successful firm ensures a steady and often substantial income.

Sometimes a significant part of a firm's practice comes from a particular client, for example, a trade union or a large corporation. In such a case, relations with that client become very important, since the firm would suffer if the client took its business elsewhere. Some solicitors find this regular relation with clients — the feeling of "seeing them through" their problems as they buy houses, form companies, get divorced, make their wills and the rest — very satisfying.

Many solicitors work in the heart of the cities, but there are also solicitors in the suburbs. Others prefer the slower pace of a country town, and do not mind the fact that they are often faced with a variety of work and no expert colleague in the next office — the benefits of specialization are to some extent denied to the country practitioner. These firms tend to take longer to get established, but can become very successful, and there are many country solicitors, with their regular clients and pleasant country life, who would never dream of coming to the city. The suburban practice is sometimes a branch of a city office, but there are plenty of quite successful solicitors in the suburbs, usually in small firms and specializing in conveyancing and other non-litigious work.

Barristers

Where do barristers fit into all this? Firstly, in the litigation cases. Unless the matter is a small one heard in a minor court — and sometimes even then — the solicitor will arrange to have a barrister appear in court on the day of the trial. But the solicitors still do a great deal of the work. They obtain statements from the witnesses, prepare the court documents, and generally prepare cases for court. Before the cases come on for hearing, the solicitors send the barristers a "brief", which is simply a bundle of all the necessary documents, tied with a ribbon (traditionally pink). Solicitors may attend "conferences" (discussions) in the barrister's chambers. When the hearing date arrives, the solicitors act in the humble role of assisting the barrister. They rush around making sure the witnesses arrive (and sometimes that they stay sober), conferring with their clients, making sure the barristers appreciate exactly what the clients want or the implication of some fact, and generally operating under the direction of the barristers, who are in charge of the conduct of the trial — subject, in theory, to the client's instructions. During the trial the solicitors do not address the court, but sit behind the barristers and sometimes assist them in whispered and hurried conversations.

There are, of course, variations in the pattern. In a difficult case, a Queen's Counsel (a senior barrister) may be engaged; if so, a "junior" will often be engaged as well, at about two-thirds of the QC's fee. Again a barrister might assist in some parts of the preparation of a case, for example to draw up some of the documents, or give advice on what sort of evidence his client should produce, and if there are settlement negotiations, the barrister will often be called in.

Secondly, barristers do quite a lot of non-litigious work. Solicitors confronted with a particularly difficult problem will often seek the client's instructions to obtain "counsel's advice". Then they will send a "brief to advise" to a barrister who (eventually) sends back an opinion. In a particularly important question the barrister might recommend that a QC's opinion be sought. This is not unlike the medical profession, where a general practitioner refers a patient to a specialist and the specialist seeks a "second opinion". The question involved might be the drafting of a complex will or some other document, advice on tax or company law, or industrial law. Any area of law can throw up a thorny legal question where a solicitor would seek counsel's advice.

Barristers do not deal with clients directly but always through solicitors. It is the solicitors who select the barristers (sometimes after discussion with the clients) and "instruct" or "brief" them to appear, and it is the solicitors who arrange for the payment of the barristers' fees. It is against the ethics of the profession for a barrister to accept work directly from a client, or to appear in court for a client without a solicitor.

Many people probably have an image of barristers arguing cases in court, looking spectacular (or perhaps absurd) in wig and gown. This is only part of the story: barristers spend much of their time in their rooms, called "chambers", working on documents. Some barristers, and often the senior ones, spend most of their time working in their chambers, in their shirt sleeves.

When barristers start out ("called to the bar") they can expect a difficult first few years. They then must obtain work from solicitors, not from the clients, and it may take a while for solicitors to get to know them and realize their ability. They will be facing new and bewildering problems and may have to solve them quickly and with no guidance. In these years, most young barristers will take any work they can get, and you will often find them appearing in the magistrates' courts dealing with less serious offences or in the District Court (or County Court) arguing civil cases involving relatively small amounts of money. They will also take on a certain amount of free work, and will probably be working harder than ever before, because they know that the reputations they are building up in these first years will make or break them. "Reputation" here refers to their image among lawyers, particularly solicitors. If successful, they will start to receive briefs of a particular kind, and may find themselves specialists in some field — family law, workers' compensation, criminal law, or whatever.

Barristers' work and professional life are somewhat different from solicitors'. Although they may go to country courts "on circuit", their chambers will be in the city near the law courts, probably in a building full of other barristers. They will practise on their own (barristers are not permitted to form partnerships) but will mix a great deal with other barristers and probably benefit greatly from the very close and comradely spirit that seems to survive the intense competitiveness of the bar. As they become established, they may well make quite a lot of money, but will find it difficult to avoid heavy income tax, and if they become ill or retire they will have no practice to sell.

Barristers' contact with clients is usually brief, though in complex and important cases they may have a series of conferences with them before the actual hearing. But sometimes they will meet them for the first time the morning of a case, or the day before, and will never see them again after the case is over. Yet during that time they might have played a decisive part in a difficult and important crisis in the client's life: perhaps a divorce, or a serious criminal case, or an action to recover compensation for a serious injury.

Successful barristers have to decide whether to "take silk". This means becoming a "Queen's Counsel", one of the senior members of the bar. If they do, they will charge higher fees, and will normally appear in cases with a "junior" barrister (that is, ones who are not QC's), assisting them. Clients will then have to decide whether they are good enough to justify this extra expense; and the decision to take silk is therefore often a difficult one, for clients who have briefed a barrister regularly in the past might now find him or her (and a junior), too expensive. The period after taking silk might be a precarious one, but a barrister who succeeds here can earn a great deal of money indeed, and perhaps after a while the offer of a judicial appointment.

The Legal Profession

The traditional division of the profession into solicitors and barristers has its roots in early English legal history. In some Australian States it has been abolished or modified by statute; only in New South Wales and Queensland has it been left untouched. However, in the other States, an interesting and surprising development has occurred (in some States more than others). Although there are formally no "solicitors" or "barristers" but only lawyers, those lawyers have tended to divide up functionally in a way that is very much the same as the old division. Some lawyers tend to specialize in court appearances, and act, in effect, as barristers, while the others do the work of solicitors; informally, and spontaneously, the "lawyers" have tended to become solicitors and barristers again. This phenomenon does not seem to have occurred in other countries where the profession has been amalgamated, for example in the United States, and is open to a variety of interpretations. It may mean that Australian lawyers just cannot change their habits, or that the traditional division is a useful one after all (at least for the lawyers). The desirability of a divided profession is in fact controversial; some regard it as a sensible specialization of skills, others argue that it leads to unnecessary duplication of work and increases the delay and expense of legal services.

Where there remains a legal split in the profession, each branch has its own professional organization. The barristers organize themselves into a "Bar", headed by a Bar Council, the presidency of which is a highly prestigious office. The solicitors have a "Law Society", or "Law Institute". These organizations, among other things, police the ethical codes of the profession by taking action (either in the Supreme Court or in special disciplinary tribunals) to have offenders "struck off the rolls" (forbidden to practise) or suspended from practice for a period, fined, or reprimanded. It is not possible here to set out these ethical rules, but to a large extent they stem from the fact that lawyers regard themselves as owing a duty to the court as well as to their clients. The rules are necessary partly because lawyers often handle large amounts of their clients' money in transactions where there are many opportunities for dishonesty or sharp practice, and partly because lawyers can find themselves in tricky situations where there is a conflict between their clients' interest and the interest of the community in the proper administration of the law. The proceedings in which lawyers are struck off for unprofessional practice are occasionally reported in the media, and the practices that come to light are often startling. The public is perhaps too ready to look on these cases as isolated instances which do not indicate any general cause for alarm; the truth is that nobody really knows how widespread such practices are, and how effective the professional organizations are in stamping them out.

Apart from such proceedings, dissatisfied clients have some remedies of their own; they can, for example, sue their solicitor for negligence or have the solicitor's bill of costs examined by an officer of the court to see if it is fair. This last remedy is a good example of a right which is not often used because few people know it exists — and lawyers are often not anxious to tell them. Curiously, the client cannot sue barristers for professional incompetence in the conduct of litigation; even if the barrister commits outrageous blunders which lose the client's case, the barrister is entirely protected from any proceedings by the client. (All other professional people — doctors, architects, etc — can be sued for professional negligence.) This rule was decided by the English House of Lords in a case in 1967, *Rondel v Worsley*, on policy grounds that we and many others find unconvincing, and even *The Times* muttered darkly in an editorial that the law knows how to look after its own. But in *Giannarelli and Others v Wraith* (1988) the High Court, by a 4-3 majority, decided to follow the House of Lords decision.

The legal profession has traditionally been governed by rules about the way lawyers should function. For example, they have been forbidden to advertise and to compete with each other by lowering fees. In addition, lawyers have a monopoly: generally speaking, it is illegal for non-lawyers to do legal work.

In former times, all this was defended as being necessary to protect the high standards of professional practice. More recently, against the background of some suspicion of professionals and the increasing use of law to discourage monopolies and unfair trading, many of these rules have come under scrutiny. Some see them as having more to do with protecting members of the legal profession than with protecting the public against unprofessional conduct, and have pointed out that they may tend to limit the availability of legal services to the public. For example, the rule that lawyers should not reduce their costs for competitive reasons tends to keep costs high. The same applies to the rule that QCs should not act unless a junior barrister, who is to be paid two-thirds the QC's fee, is also engaged. Again, the rule that lawyers cannot advertise may prevent members of the public from finding out which firms include non-English speaking lawyers, and which firms are competent in specialised areas such as immigration law.

The legal profession, like other professions, has been affected by the pressure to change, and some of the rules mentioned have been considerably modified in recent years. For example, restrictions on advertising by solicitors have been relaxed in most parts of Australia. (Barristers are more restricted; indeed there is still a rule in some States that they cannot indicate in the telephone directory that they are barristers.) The former restrictions on price cutting and some other forms of attracting business have also been relaxed.

In 1982 the New South Wales Law Reform Commission published a major Report on the legal profession and its organisation. The Report sought to balance two important objectives: having an independent legal profession, and yet having some way of ensuring that the profession would be responsive to the needs of the community, and would not merely advance the interests of its members. It recommended considerable changes, involving a move towards public accountability through community participation on the key professional bodies. The Report also supported the relaxation of the traditional rules that had tended to limit effective access by the public to legal services. Not surprisingly, the Report was controversial, but there is no doubt that it has played a significant part in the process of change that has taken place in recent times. It was not until 1987 that legislation was passed implementing some of the Commission's proposals. Weisbrot comments that to date the legal professions have been "very successful in resisting external (including State) intervention in reforming the structures and practices of legal work, in particular in warding off efforts to diminish the degree of self-regulation and to merge the large divided professions in the eastern States". It remains to be seen whether it can continue to do so. As we write, in 1992, issues relating to the legal profession are again being reviewed by the Commission, and the legal profession in New South Wales appears to be losing its former monopoly over conveyancing.

Reorganization of the legal profession is a complex and slow business, usually opposed by lawyers themselves. Even if reorganization and reform does prevail, however, it is unlikely to make fundamental changes in the sort of work lawyers do and the sort of clients they mostly serve.

A great many top lawyers specialize in protecting the property interests of the well-to-do in the community; taxation and company law provide some of the most sophisticated law and lawyers in the country. But criminal law, particularly in the lower courts, is much less developed; thus poor people facing criminal charges have cruder law and less legal assistance than rich people have in reducing their income tax. Children's Courts see a sad line of mystified children facing proceedings that can make or mar their entire lives. For thousands of people "property" consists of social security benefits of one kind or another, but the systems under which these benefits are distributed are still not well known to most lawyers, and these people have little legal assistance in securing just treatment under a highly complex and technical system which many of them cannot understand.

Lawyers may stress the importance of their role in maintaining the rule of law and representing the rights of citizens, and there is some truth in this. But much of what lawyers do, and most of what the best lawyers do, has to do with advancing the interests of corporations and rich people. Part of the reason for this may be that, as we have seen, most lawyers come from relatively secure and well-educated sections of the community and may be unfamiliar or unsympathetic with the problems of the more depressed sections.

Another part of the answer may have to do with the "occupational hazards" of the professional life of a lawyer. It is a very *institutional* life. Lawyers are continually working within the context of courts, legislatures, prisons, government departments, and the rest, and they look for solutions to their clients' problems in terms of those institutions and the values and practices they have. This may make it difficult for lawyers to see the system as a whole and evaluate its effectiveness in achieving its goals (let alone evaluate those goals themselves). We shall return to this issue in Chapter 11, when we discuss legal aid and access to justice.

Lawyers are professionally trained to look to the past to solve problems; as we saw in Chapter 4, much of the law has been built up through the backwards-looking technique of precedent. This approach provides a valuable element of stability in society but could be a liability in those parts of society where rapid change is called for.

Lawyers are used to working with prescribed solutions — what a previous judge, or a statute says — and they deal with a limited range of facts; those that are "relevant" according to the highly technical rules of evidence. There is an obvious danger that they may never find those solutions which are unfamiliar, or discover those facts which don't fit the system but may be all important.

Lawyers almost invariably address themselves to be the needs of individual clients, not of the public generally. The lawyer will ask whether the client is entitled to a divorce, or to compensation for an accident, but will seldom have to ask (in professional life) whether the law of divorce is satisfactory to the public, or whether the basis for recovery for accidents is a just one. Taking wider perspectives on social issues may not be particularly useful in the day-to-day work of most lawyers. As David Weisbrot says, "where philosophers aspire to Grand Theory, lawyers aspire to The Loophole". As a result, lawyers are not necessarily well qualified to determine policies on matters of general social importance, including, perhaps, general issues relating to legal services, such as whether conveyancing should be a monopoly of the legal profession.

Finally, lawyers spend much of their time *telling* people what the law is, what is "relevant", what they can and cannot do, how they should put their story; and they do this in a setting which is familiar to them but is often strange and frightening to their clients. All this telling may tend to make lawyers arrogant and insensitive, and make them confuse what is effective within the system with what is beneficial in a more general sense for the society, or for individuals.

This is somewhat speculative, but lawyers occupy a powerful position in the community and their capacity to contribute to it will depend in part on their capacity to recognise and understand changing community needs. It is possible to identify a number of emerging changes in the concerns of our societies which will compel changes in law and in lawyers; the increasing sophistication of commercial transactions, particularly at the international level; increasing governmental regulation and control of various aspects of life; recognition of the need to protect and even to improve the physical environment; the need to secure greater social justice for disadvantaged members of society (racial minorities, the poor, the elderly, etc); the need to conserve dwindling resources; a rising concern for individual rights and liberties. Finally, and most immediately, lawyers will need to help tackle the enormous problems of access to justice caused partly by high costs and fees associated with the adversary system: we explore this issue further in Chapter 11.

In the future, we may expect that there will be less need for lawyers in the buying and selling of land and houses — a computerized registry should be able greatly to simplify this area of work. Claims for compensation for accidents, particularly road accidents, will consume far less legal effort when systems of no-fault compensation are eventually established. These two developments will remove a large amount of lucrative work for lawyers.

On the other hand lawyers will need to develop new approaches and new skills to deal effectively with tribunals concerned with exercises of administrative power. There will be a growing need in Australia for a new style of "public interest" legal practice to provide legal services for the disadvantaged, to support the consumer interest against big corporations and governments, and to participate actively in the broader function of law reform. The beginnings of such trends are already apparent. Unless one envisages a future Utopia which will have no need for lawyers, or unless lawyers are to become irrelevant to emerging social needs, we will need a better understanding of the characteristics of lawyers, and a better appraisal of the effectiveness with which the law and lawyers fulfil the various functions which society has a right to expect of them.

9
Courts of Law

In this chapter we give a brief account of the Australian system of courts, or more precisely, the different systems of courts for the States and Commonwealth.

Until the 1980s, it could not quite be called an *Australian* system, because the top court in the hierarchy was in London: it was the Judicial Committee of the Privy Council. This body, whose membership largely coincided with that of the House of Lords in its judicial capacity, used to have jurisdiction to hear appeals from decisions of Australian courts, and also of the courts of New Zealand, Malaysia, Singapore, Hong Kong and several other Commonwealth nations and "colonies". As a result of several legislative amendments, culminating in the *Australia Act* 1986, (Cth) and the *Australia Act* 1986, (UK) appeals to the Privy Council from Australia have been terminated. Privy Council decisions may still be referred to in Australian courts but they are no longer binding precedents. With the passing of this relic of colonialism we can accurately refer to the *Australian* system of courts.

State Courts

(a) Inferior Courts

All States have a lower level of courts presided over by magistrates or Justices of the Peace. These courts are held ("sit") in particular areas in the State and normally have jurisdiction (power to hear and determine cases) within their respective areas. They have both criminal and civil jurisdiction in minor matters, and carry out a variety of other functions. The criminal jurisdiction is kept separate from the civil, and often the court will operate under a different name, even though the same magistrate may preside over both types of case. Of course, the powers and procedures will be different according to whether the proceedings are civil or criminal. Magistrates generally try cases alone, not with a jury.

When exercising *civil jurisdiction*, the courts have various names in different States, for example, *Magistrates' Courts, Local Courts* and *Courts of Requests*. The civil cases include minor disputes in the "common law" area and some specialized matters under State statutes such as landlord and tenant disputes and hire purchase, or under federal legislation, notably the *Family Law Act* 1975. The proceedings are relatively quick, inexpensive and, for legal proceedings, informal. There is only limited provision for appeal, so that (1) the disputes can be settled finally as soon as possible and (2) the higher courts will not be bothered with the "minor" disputes of less wealthy people. In civil cases, the court's jurisdiction is usually limited to cases where the amount claimed or the value of the property at stake is less than a certain figure, which (as usual) differs from State to State.

When exercising *criminal jurisdiction* the courts are known as *Magistrates' Courts*, or *Courts of Petty Sessions*, or *Courts of Summary Jurisdiction*. Another name formerly used was Police Courts, which is inaccurate in so far as it suggests that the magistrate is a police officer; this is not so, but with the large number of uniformed police in the courts, giving evidence, ushering people in and out, prosecuting cases and assisting the business of the court, it is an understandable description.

In their criminal jurisdiction the courts have power to try and to impose sentence in summary offences under State or Federal legislation. Proceedings in summary trials are generally quicker than in trial by judge and jury (which is the form of trial for "indictable" as opposed to summary offences) and the penalties are less. There are provisions for appeal to higher courts, especially where the complaint is that the magistrate made a mistake of law.

An important part of the courts' criminal jurisdiction is the conduct of preliminary hearings or "committal proceedings" in respect of indictable offences, that is, serious offences, tried by judge and jury. This is discussed further in Chapter 10.

Another function of these busy courts may be to act as a *Coroner's Court*. The ancient English office of Coroner is normally conferred in Australia on magistrates or Justices of the Peace. The main function of a Coroner's Court is to hold an inquiry or inquest into unexplained deaths, for example, where a person has died a violent or unnatural death, or under suspicious or unusual circumstances, or from unknown causes. Coroners also have power to hold inquests into the cause and origin of fires which have destroyed or damaged property, and in Queensland they may also hold inquiries in regard to missing persons. Proceedings in Coroners' Courts are similar, at first sight, to those of ordinary courts. They are usually open to the public, and witnesses may be summoned and examined on oath. In all States except Queensland and South Australia there is provision for the inquest to be held with a jury in certain circumstances. But such inquests are not really judicial proceedings at all. They are simply to investigate facts, for example, to establish the identity of a deceased person and when, how and why he or she died. They may of course produce information on the basis of which some person may be charged with an offence; if so, the Coroners (in most jurisdictions) may then go on to commit that person for trial.

In each State a special type of jurisdiction conferred on some magistrates is the jurisdiction exercised under the name of *Children's Courts*. These courts can try summarily offences charged against persons under a specified age (which varies from State to State), even indictable offences (other than the most serious offences such as murder). They may also commit young offenders for trial in a higher court. Charges of certain offences against young persons, and certain proceedings regarding the welfare of young persons, are also heard in these courts. Children's Courts are not normally open to the public. The main purpose in having special courts of this type is to protect children from the publicity and other undesirable features of trial in the ordinary courts, and to allow the court to make any of a wide range of orders for the welfare of the child.

One way and another, magistrates and Justices of the Peace play a very significant role in the administration of the law. Their jurisdiction covers a wide and diverse field, and their decisions vitally affect the lives of those who come before them. For example, where they sit as Children's Courts they have the widest powers over the lives of children who are alleged to have committed offences or to be in need of care or protection, and their decisions turn on subtle and elusive questions: will the child's welfare be better served by leaving him or her in a difficult family situation or by a placement elsewhere? And how should the child's welfare be balanced against the interests of society in preserving the peace or protecting the property of individuals?

And yet, perhaps because they tend to deal with less wealthy and important people in the community, magistrates and their courts are generally poor in terms of prestige, legal training, pay, and facilities, and are firmly at the bottom of the legal system.

(b) Intermediate Courts

All States except Tasmania provide for an intermediate level of courts between those presided over by magistrates or Justices of the Peace and the Supreme Court. The presiding officer is a judge, who generally has jurisdiction over both civil and criminal cases.

Intermediate *criminal* courts are known as District Courts, District Criminal Courts (SA), or (in Victoria) County Courts. These Courts try indictable offences with the assistance of a jury, though the more serious of these offences are generally tried in the Supreme Court. They may also hear appeals from conviction or sentence of lower criminal courts.

Intermediate *civil* courts are also known as District Courts or (in Victoria) County Courts. The same judges will normally be involved in both civil and criminal jurisdictions. The jurisdiction is primarily in common law disputes, subject to an upper limit of money claimed or property involved which varies from one State or type of dispute to another. There may also be limited equity jurisdiction and jurisdiction conferred by statutes dealing with particular topics. They may also have some power to hear appeals from lower courts and tribunals.

The function of these intermediate courts, where they exist, is to relieve Supreme Courts of much of their business and to allow such actions to be dealt with in the appropriate part of the State; intermediate court judges travel to country centres to hear cases more often than Supreme Court judges do. Proceedings are more formal than those in Magistrates' Courts.

(c) Supreme Courts

In each State (and for each Territory) there is a Supreme Court consisting of a Chief Justice and a number of other "puisne" judges. ("Puisne" is pronounced "puny" and is the subject of many mispronunciations and bad jokes.) Some of these judges may specialize, to a greater or lesser degree, in a particular sort of work. The Court has both civil and criminal jurisdiction.

The Supreme Courts have both "original" and "appellate" jurisdiction. The original jurisdiction, that is, the hearing of a case at first instance, is generally exercised by a single judge, either in the State capital or on circuit in other parts of the State. Their jurisdiction is general, but usually only the more serious criminal cases or the more important civil disputes at common law come before the Supreme Courts at first instance; the others are heard mostly in inferior or intermediate courts, from which they may be taken to the Supreme Court on appeal or review. But in non common law matters (for example, equity, probate, etc) little or no jurisdiction is given to inferior or intermediate courts. Some of the jurisdiction exercised by State Supreme Courts is Federal jurisdiction, that is, jurisdiction conferred on such courts by Commonwealth legislation.

The jurisdiction of Supreme Courts to review decisions of a single Supreme Court judge, lower courts or other State tribunals, by appeal or some other procedure, is generally exercised by a "Full Court" consisting of several Supreme Court judges (or, in New South Wales, a specialist Court of Appeal). In criminal cases such a court may be known as the Court of Criminal Appeal.

Federal Courts

(a) The High Court of Australia

The High Court has original jurisdiction in a number of matters listed in s 75 of the Commonwealth Constitution. It also has some additional original jurisdiction conferred on it by Parliament in matters listed in s 76 of the Constitution. The most important matters are constitutional cases. Some of the listed matters may be heard only in the High Court; others may be heard in State courts or the Federal Court. The original jurisdiction of the High Court is generally exercised by a single judge.

The High Court also has an appellate jurisdiction which is not confined to specific types of matters. It may hear appeals from decisions of State or Territory Supreme Courts whether exercising State or Federal jurisdiction, or of other Federal Courts, or of other courts exercising Federal jurisdiction, or of the High Court itself in its original jurisdiction. Appellate jurisdiction is normally exercised by three or more judges. When the appeal concerns the constitutional powers of the Commonwealth it is heard by all seven High Court judges. There is no further appeal from the High Court. The High Court is located in Canberra but occasionally sits in State capitals.

The High Court's importance lies both in its role as the primary custodian of the Constitution and also in its role (over 90 per cent of its caseload) as a general court of appeal for Australia. Professor James Crawford, in his excellent book *Australian Courts of Law*, comments:

> The High Court is the most visible, and arguably the most important, court in Australia. This is not so much because of the number of cases it decides or (at least in non-constitutional cases) because of the effect of its orders on litigants. It is because of the indirect effects of its judgments, as precedents determining the result of other cases in other courts, as authoritative statements of the law (it takes eight Acts of Parliament to reverse the effect of a single High Court decision on a

matter of common law over which the Commonwealth Parliament has no authority), as an expression of position on sensitive political or social questions.

(b) Other Federal Courts

Although the Commonwealth Parliament has generally chosen to vest Federal jurisdiction (other than that of the High Court) in existing State Courts, it has also created some special Federal Courts. The most important, until the 1970s, (when they were abolished) were the *Federal Court of Bankruptcy* and the *Industrial Court*. In 1976 the Commonwealth Parliament established the *Family Court of Australia* and the *Federal Court of Australia*.

The *Federal Court* consists of divisions: an Industrial Division, replacing the Australian Industrial Court; and a General Division which comprises bankruptcy jurisdiction plus jurisdiction under a number of federal statutes in areas such as trade practices and administrative law. The Federal Court also has appellate jurisdiction to hear appeals from decisions of a single judge of the Federal Court, from Territory Supreme Courts, from State Courts in certain federal matters (for example, copyright, taxation) and from certain other decisions. Further appeal may lie to the High Court.

The establishment of the Federal Court and the Family Court has given rise to some very difficult questions as to whether they or State Courts are the right courts to hear certain sorts of cases. There has been much debate about the problems of a dual system of courts and of the advantages of achieving some sort of unified court structure for Australia. The problems have been somewhat reduced by a system of "cross-vesting" legislation which was passed by the Commonwealth and the States in 1987 and came into force in 1988. This system allows certain courts, notably the State Supreme Courts and federal courts, to exercise each other's jurisdiction.

(c) Territory Courts

The Commonwealth Parliament has also established Supreme Courts and inferior courts for Commonwealth territories — the Australian Capital Territory, Northern Territory, etc. It has done so under its power in Constitution s 122 to make laws for the Territories.

Specialized Courts and Tribunals

It is worth noting at this point the existence in the Australian legal system of special courts or bodies outside the ordinary court system already outlined. Such courts or tribunals may be set up under Commonwealth or State laws, usually to decide matters which may arise in the administration of some particular area of government or some particular sorts of private transactions.

A State may have an Industrial Court or Commission to settle industrial disputes and to regulate conditions in industry, a Public Service Board or Commission to control the public service, Workers' Compensation Boards, censorship boards, planning authorities, small claims courts or tribunals, anti-discrimination boards, rent tribunals, marketing boards, liquor licensing tribunals and many others.

Commonwealth specialized courts and tribunals include the Family Court of Australia, the Administrative Appeals Tribunal, the Australian Conciliation and Arbitration Commission, the Trade Practices Tribunal, the Industries Assistance Commission, the Australian Broadcasting Tribunal, and many others.

Such tribunals frequently have functions very similar to those of the ordinary courts. But Commonwealth tribunals are not permitted to have any power which can be classified as "judicial", because of the separation of judicial power laid down in ss 71 and 72 of the Commonwealth Constitution. There is no similar limitation in regard to State tribunals.

There are hundreds of tribunals in the country today. They are established by different statutes, for different purposes, and their composition, powers and procedures show great variety. There has been no attempt in Australia to impose any sort of common standards until recently. The Commonwealth Parliament is now imposing some system at Federal level, as discussed in Chapter 12. Some of these different functions may at State level be vested in courts (often Magistrates' Courts). Sometimes judges of the State Supreme Court or an intermediate court, or magistrates or practising lawyers, may be appointed as chairpersons; otherwise the body may consist of non-lawyers, often experts in the particular field or representatives of interests most closely affected.

The procedures of tribunals may be very informal. At the other extreme they may be similar to those followed by courts, sometimes because this is required by statute, sometimes by choice.

There may or may not be statutory provision for appeal from the decisions of a tribunal to a higher tribunal or to a court. But even if there is no such provision, frequently the superior courts (Supreme Courts, Federal Court or High Court) may still review a decision if there has been any serious irregularity in the proceedings.

10
Due Process of Law

The fifth Amendment to the Constitution of the United States of America provides that "no person shall be ... deprived of life, liberty or property without due process of law".

Article 10 of the Universal Declaration of Human Rights provides that "everyone is entitled to a fair and public hearing by an independent and impartial tribunal, in the determination of his rights and obligations and of any criminal charge against him".

The requirement of fair trial is one of the basic elements in "the rule of law". In the United States the requirement has superior status under the Constitution so that any statute which allows for a person's rights to be affected other than by due process of law will be invalid.

In Australia, however, as in Britain, due process of law is not guaranteed by the Constitution. For the most part, Parliaments may, if they choose, make laws providing for people to be thrown into dungeons, and so forth without due process. The only limiting factor in Australia is s 71 of the Commonwealth Constitution which provides that if any such power to affect people under Commonwealth law can be classified as judicial, it may be vested only in the High Court or other Federal court constituted in accordance with s 72, or in State courts. If the power can be classified in some other way, for example, as administrative, then it may validly be given to some other tribunal or a Minister or public servant. (There is quite a lot of technical law on the question whether a power is to be classified as judicial.) Under State law, there is no limitation of this sort, even for judicial powers.

The legal notion of due process of law takes the procedures of the courts as a model. These procedures, developed over the centuries, are the main subject of this chapter.

When legislation gives powers to a public official or body other than a court, it often requires that person or body to follow procedures similar to those of the courts. Even if it does not, the courts can themselves sometimes review the decisions and proceedings on the basis of some element of procedural unfairness, as mentioned in Chapter 12.

The principle of due process of law, therefore, is part of our legal system in that it governs courts; it is (sometimes) embodied in legislation; and it is (sometimes) accepted by courts in reviewing the proceedings of lower courts, tribunals and officials, even where Parliament has not expressly required a fair hearing.

The requirements of due process are most fully developed in the procedures of the courts, and although the law often requires other bodies (for example, trade unions or organs of local government) to conduct fair hearings into certain matters, the procedures are much less elaborate and formal than those of the courts. The notion of due process and a fair trial in the Australian legal system is therefore best understood through an examination of the procedures of the courts.

We do not propose to analyse court procedures in detail. They are complex, and vary from one type of court or one jurisdiction to another. Instead we will discuss the basic principles which underlie court procedures in our system. It is worth noting that procedures are strictest in criminal proceedings when the liberty of the accused may be at stake.

The fundamental rule of "due process" and "natural justice" is that no person shall be judged unheard. There must be a hearing, and the hearing must be fair. How do Australian courts achieve these objectives?

Notice

If there is to be a hearing, the person who may be affected must, obviously, have sufficient notice of the fact. If it is to be a fair hearing he or she must also know in advance the case to be answered.

In *civil* proceedings at common law this is achieved by an exchange of documents between the parties.

Suppose you are punched by your neighbour, Fred. You prepare a document setting out your side of the story: how it happened, the injuries you suffered, and the amount of damages you claim. You have this document "issued" by a court officer (who stamps it) and then "served" on the defendant (you give it to Fred). Fred then prepares a document setting out his side of the story, and goes through the same process of issuing and serving it on you. He may, perhaps, deny that he punched you; or he may admit the punch but say it was in self-defence. You can then respond to that, by denying that you had attacked him. So it goes, until the documents make it clear what is really in dispute: it may be whether Fred punched you at all, or it may be whether you had attacked him first. When this stage arrives, it is said that "issue is joined", and the case can then be put on the list for hearing. The point of the whole exercise — a kind of paper war — is to avoid misunderstanding and waste of time, as well as to help each side prepare for the trial. For example, if Fred admits punching you there is no need to bother calling evidence to prove it: the only evidence necessary is that relating to the question of self-defence. In most cases, the documents are drafted by lawyers. They can be very long and complicated, for example in complex commercial cases in the higher courts, but in the lower courts they are usually less elaborate.

In *criminal* proceedings the procedures are different. Fred may be arrested by police and charged with the alleged offence. For less serious offences, he may be summonsed instead. He is entitled to full particulars of the charge against him, and the court may order that he be given such particulars.

If Fred is charged with an indictable offence (that is, one of the more serious offences that needs to be tried by judge and jury) then a preliminary hearing (or "committal proceeding") must be held before a magistrate as soon as possible. In the meantime, he may be released on bail, unless the Court feels that he may abscond, commit another offence, or try to get at witnesses, or unless the offence is particularly serious, for example, murder.

At the preliminary hearing the Crown produces its evidence in order to establish that it has a plausible ("prima facie") case against Fred. If the evidence seems insufficient to warrant putting him to trial, the magistrate may discharge him; otherwise he will be committed for trial. Fred may himself give evidence and call witnesses at the preliminary hearing, but in most cases he will not do so. As a result of the preliminary hearing, Fred has learnt not only the charge he has to answer but also the evidence the Crown will be relying on. The Crown, on the other hand, usually has little knowledge of what defence the accused will raise, or what sort of evidence he will be calling. This is why Fred chose not to give evidence at this stage.

So, in civil cases each side is entitled to full notice of the opponent's case (though not the evidence to be called). In criminal cases, however, while the accused is entitled to prior notice of the prosecution's case (and, where there is a committal proceeding, also its evidence) the prosecution has no similar right to notice of the accused's defence. This apparent bias is partly because the prosecution has many advantages, and partly because of the traditional view that it is essential to prevent innocent people being convicted, even at the expense of some guilty people going free.

Publicity

It is an important principle that judicial proceedings should normally be conducted in open court, so that members of the public, including press representatives, may attend if they wish to do so. Article 10 of the Universal Declaration of Human Rights requires "a fair *and public* hearing". It is felt that because there is a vital public interest in the administration of justice, it should be treated as a public matter, even though a particular case involves only the affairs of private individuals.

There are exceptions. Minor aspects of cases may be settled in private chambers or closed court. A judge may close a court to the public if they are disrupting the proceedings, or if a witness is unable to give evidence in open court, or if evidence to be given is of a secret nature, for example, where it relates to security matters or secret industrial processes. Children's Courts are commonly closed to the public.

In some cases, although the public's access to the courts is not affected, restrictions are imposed on what may be published in the press or elsewhere. Thus evidence in family law cases may not be published.

Apart from these exceptional cases, if court proceedings are not conducted openly they may be held to be invalid.

Standards of Proof

As a general rule, any person seeking some kind of court order must provide the court with a good reason for making the order. This obvious principle is reflected in the law. The plaintiff in civil proceedings and the prosecution in criminal proceedings must succeed in proving their case to the court, showing either that they are entitled to some remedy or that the defendant has committed some offence. In legal terms, the plaintiff and the prosecution bear the "onus of proof". But another question is: how strongly must the case be proved? How sure does the court have to be before it makes an order? The answer to this question is different in civil and criminal cases.

In *civil* cases, a plaintiff simply has to persuade the court — judge or jury — that the facts he or she alleges are true on a *reasonable balance of probabilities*. If after hearing both sides, the judge or jury feels that the plaintiff's story is more likely than not to be true, then the plaintiff will be entitled to a verdict.

In *criminal* cases, the standard of proof is much stricter. It is a fundamental principle of the common law system, expressed also in Article 11 of the Universal Declaration of Human Rights, that a person is presumed to be innocent until proved guilty. The prosecution has to do much more than to tip the "scales of justice" its way; it must prove the accused's guilt *beyond all reasonable doubt*. No matter how strong the prosecution's evidence may be, if the magistrate or the jury has any reasonable doubt that he or she is guilty, the accused is entitled to be acquitted.

Evidence

The decision of a case where facts are in dispute can only be based on evidence as to those facts. No evidence is admissible in court proceedings unless it is *relevant* to the issue in question. If you were being tried on a charge of offensive behaviour arising out of a street demonstration, it would be irrelevant for the prosecution to produce evidence that you had been charged with evading bus fares three years earlier. That evidence would be "inadmissible": the court would not allow it to be given.

The rules of evidence are complex. They are designed to keep out evidence which is irrelevant, and evidence which might be relevant but would unfairly prejudice a party. The rules are particularly strict in criminal cases.

We will not go into details, but simply give a few examples:

(a) Frieda is on trial for fraud. She made a full confession at the police station, but pleads not guilty and says she only made the confession because she was frightened of being assaulted by the police. The courts will only admit it as evidence if it was made voluntarily, and not if any threat or promise had been made to get it. Furthermore, the judges may not admit such a statement as evidence if Frieda had not first been warned by the police that she was under no obligation to say anything, and that anything she did say might be used as evidence.

The police sometimes complain that these strict requirements hamstring investigation of crime, that innocent persons have nothing to fear in speaking up, and that the rules protect only the guilty by warning them to say nothing. They would like to see the rules modified in some way without jeopardizing the rights of the innocent, but others see them as essential in the interests of civil liberty.

(b) Evidence is not admissible in criminal proceedings to show that the accused has had previous convictions or is of bad character. The sole issue is whether he or she is guilty of the specific offence.

However, evidence of character and previous convictions is admissible after a person has been found guilty, in order to assist the magistrate or judge to impose the appropriate sentence.

(c) Hearsay evidence is inadmissible. Janet is on trial for murder. Andrew, an eye-witness, can say: "I saw the blood stained-knife in Janet's hand". However, Martin cannot say "Andrew told me he saw the blood-stained knife in Janet's hand". Martin's statement is inadmissible because it is considered less reliable than first-hand evidence, and because Janet (the accused) should have the opportunity to cross-examine Andrew in court.

These and other rules of evidence are an important safeguard for fair trial.

Each party has a right to give evidence, usually in the form of oral evidence by witnesses in court. The other party also has a right to cross-examine those witnesses, by asking questions in order to discover other facts, or in order to diminish the weight of the evidence already given. If anything new comes out of cross-examination, the first party may re-examine.

Generally, no evidence or information may be presented to the court in the absence or "behind the back" of the other side. The common law technique of examining witnesses by question and answer is designed to give the other side time to object in order to keep out inadmissible evidence.

Impartiality

So far we have seen that our court procedures aim to ensure that both parties can present their cases to the court as fully and as fairly as possible. This, however, will not ensure a fair trial if the court itself is biased.

We have already considered, in Chapter 8, the means by which the general independence of judges is achieved. They have independence and security of tenure, immunity from legal liability for things said or done in judicial proceedings, and so should fear no pressures from Government or anyone else.

A problem of impartiality may arise, though, in a particular case. For example, you may be suing a company and the judge may be a shareholder in that company. You may be suing your next door neighbour for allowing his incinerator to get out of control so that it burnt down your garage, and the judge may turn out to be the neighbour's cousin. You may be a Ruritanian migrant, and the judge may have said, in an earlier case, that he had always found Ruritanian migrants to be untruthful.

In each of these and similar cases, if the judge did not stand down willingly, you could object to that judge hearing the case. It is a fundamental principle that "people may not be judges in their own cause", and this will disqualify a judge from hearing a case in which he or she has some financial or personal interest, or in which other circumstances exist so as to raise a reasonable suspicion of bias. It is not necessary to show that the judge is in fact biased — a reasonable suspicion is enough. To quote the famous words of a former English Lord Chief Justice: "Justice should not only be done but should manifestly and undoubtedly be seen to be done".

Indictable criminal cases, and some civil cases too, are tried not by a judge alone but by a judge and jury. The jury in such a case decides the facts. The possibility of bias among the jurors is sought to be met by provisions for "challenge". Both parties have a right to challenge members of the jury panel if they think that they are biased against them for one reason or another. They may dismiss a certain number of jurors without giving a reason; beyond that point they must give a reason for challenge. The details vary from one type of case to another, and from one state or territory to another. Generally, the opportunity to challenge jurors is greater in criminal than in civil cases.

Trial by Jury

The use of jury trial is itself a special and characteristic feature of the common law system. It is used for all indictable criminal offences, except where there is an option to have the offence tried summarily by a magistrate, and the option is taken. It is also used for the trial of some civil actions at common law.

When jury trial is available, the effect is that the determination of facts and the weighing up of evidence is entrusted to a group of one's fellow citizens rather than to a judge. The system has a long history and has considerable emotional overtones in our society, at least in criminal cases.

No special qualifications are needed for jury service. Usually entry on the electoral roll is sufficient. Different classes of persons may be exempt from service, for example, doctors, teachers, members of Parliament, lawyers, and others. Individuals may apply for exemption for personal reasons, for example, illness, or insufficient command of the English language. The actual jury for a case is selected, by ballot and after challenges, from a larger number summoned to the court.

In criminal cases a jury of 12 is used. It hears the evidence, listens to addresses of counsel for both sides, and to the judge's summing-up. The judge directs them, in accordance with the law, as to what verdict they should return on various possible conclusions they may reach about the facts. For example, in a murder case the judge might tell them that if they find that A did kill B and did so with deliberate intent, then they will return a verdict of guilty; if they find that A killed B but did so in self-defence or under provocation, they shall return a verdict of not guilty of murder but guilty of manslaughter; if they have any reasonable doubt whether A killed B at all, they should return a verdict of not guilty.

The jury then retires and, when it reaches a decision, delivers its verdict to the court. Traditionally criminal verdicts have to be unanimous and, if the jury fails to agree on a verdict, they are discharged and a new trial must be held. But in England and some Australian States provision has now been made to receive verdicts of a large majority of the jurors in some circumstances after a specified time.

If the jury finds the accused not guilty, he or she is acquitted, and can never again be tried for the same offence. If the jury returns a verdict of "guilty", the judge then imposes sentence.

The task of the criminal jury, then, is to decide facts in the light of the law as put to them by the judge.

The size of civil juries varies from one State to another, and there are possible variations within States. Civil jury verdicts do not have to be unanimous, and the decision of a specified majority may be accepted after a certain time. Jury trial is not available in all civil cases, even in common law matters. In recent years, both in Australia and elsewhere, jury trials in civil cases have been giving way to trial by judges sitting alone. Juries make for longer and slower trials, and in civil cases they do not have quite the same sort of emotive support as in criminal cases.

Most civil cases tried by jury are actions for damages, whether the cause of action is negligence or defamation or something else. As in criminal cases, the civil jury listens to the evidence and returns a verdict in the light of the law as put to them by the judge, but normally they must then go on to assess the amount of damages (if any) which the defendant should pay. In criminal cases, the judge decides on sentence; in civil cases the jury decides on damages.

Appeal

The procedures mentioned do not of course guarantee that the decision of a court will be correct, on the facts or on the law. In particular, the law itself may not be clear. A further safeguard is to make provision whereby decisions may be reviewed by a higher court on several possible grounds, and by various procedures. The Australian legal system does, in fact, provide fairly amply for appeal to a higher court and, if necessary, ultimately to the High Court of Australia, if it grants special leave.

Legal Representation and the Adversary Procedure

The court-room procedure sketched above is often referred to as the "adversary system". This is a fair description, for the law courts are places where the parties fight out their cases according to the rules of the game — the rules of evidence and procedure — and they fight for a favourable judgment. The court adopts a basically passive role, reaching a decision on the evidence and arguments which the parties put before it. (There are, however, other possible procedures for resolving disputes and reviewing problems. A Royal Commission, for example, may call its own witnesses and make its own investigations: its procedure is quite different from that of a court and could be described as "inquisitorial".)

In the adversary procedure of the courts, much turns on how the parties present their cases. The law provides that any party to court proceedings is not only entitled to be heard, but also to be represented by a lawyer (if he or she can afford one). Parties themselves can of course argue their own case, even in the highest courts, but lawyers regard this as very unwise, shake their heads, and invariably make the stock witticism that "anyone who acts as his own lawyer has a fool for a client". This professional attitude is very good for business, of course, but it is probably unfair to write it off as self-serving. Legal proceedings are usually very technical, and there would be few cases which lay persons could successfully argue on their own. On the other hand, the moves towards "do it yourself" kits for undefended divorces and land transfers may indicate a growing scepticism of the lawyers' claims, and a questioning of the need for their services in some areas. Criticism along these lines goes hand in hand with calls for simplification of procedures to make the business more intelligible to non-lawyers, and lawyers' assurances that this cannot be done are not likely to continue to go unchallenged.

For all this, it remains true that legal proceedings in courts, and many legal matters outside courts, for example, drafting wills, do usually require lawyers, and laypeople would be very likely to get into serious trouble on their own. Any significant court hearing, whether civil or criminal, will involve rules of procedure and evidence which a layperson will not usually understand, and unrepresented persons in criminal or civil cases run a real risk of being prejudiced by their lack of knowledge about how the system works. (The problem presented by the inability of many people to pay for legal services is considered in the following chapter.)

The adversary procedure not only means that lawyers are usually necessary, but also places them in a position of some responsibility. The court inevitably relies on the lawyers to put their arguments fairly, and the law places certain restraints on lawyers in their efforts to advance their clients' interests. For example, lawyers must not knowingly mislead the court by making allegations which they know are false, or by deliberately failing to tell the court about a relevant precedent, even if it is unfavourable to their case. Courts place quite a deal of trust in lawyers: in an emergency, a court might make an order on the basis of allegations made by a barrister even without evidence, then adjourn the case while the evidence is collected. The working out of lawyers' responsibilities to their clients and to the courts is not simple.

The rules of procedure and evidence which make up our "due process of law" are among the most difficult and complex parts of the law. While they represent a very notable effort to minimize human error and ensure just trials, they do so at the price of substantial legal costs and delay. They also tend to make the courts mysterious and intimidating for many people. In some areas, it seems, the price is too high. For example, many commercial people try to resolve their disputes out of court if possible, often through arbitration, where lawyers need not be involved at all. In some places Community Justice Centres may be available to resolve disputes between neighbours (for example) by mediation. There have been moves to set up special courts and tribunals where small claims can be resolved quickly and sensibly without the complexities and expense which seem inevitably to accompany lawyers and courts. Some of these are discussed in Chapter 11.

11

Legal Aid and Access to Justice

The Ideal: Equal Access to Justice

> We cannot be said to live under the rule of law, in the full meaning of that expression, unless all citizens are able to assert and defend their legal rights effectively and have access to the court for that purpose. Under our legal system . . . that requires professional assistance. If that professional assistance is denied to any citizen who reasonably needs it to assert or defend his [sic] legal rights, the rule of law in the society is to that extent deficient.

This fine statement was made in 1984 by Chief Justice King of South Australia. Let's look at it. The "rule of law" stands for values which are traditionally cherished in our legal tradition. It includes the notion that official power is exercised according to law, rather than the whim or favour of those in authority. Accordingly, judges and magistrates swear oaths to "do right by all manner of people . . . without fear or favour, affection or ill-will". This idea is discussed further in Chapter 12. Chief Justice King's statement, however, emphasizes a different point about the rule of law: that all citizens should be equally able to assert or defend their legal rights. That means that everyone should be equal before the law: the powerful and the weak; the rich and the poor; the government official and the private citizen; the corporation and the individual; members of the "mainstream" society and members of racial or other minority groups; and so on.

How far does our legal system live up to this ideal? An answer to that question would require an examination not only of the rules of law contained in legislation and case-law, but also of how the system operates in practice. For example, the rules of criminal law do not generally discriminate between Aborigines and other people, yet in a famous study (*Fear Favour or Affection*, 1976) Elizabeth Eggleston demonstrated many ways in which Aboriginal people were discriminated against in the actual administration of the criminal law. Numerous later studies have confirmed this.

In this chapter, we will consider only one aspect of equality before the law, involving equal access to justice. Are the Courts and legal remedies equally available to all people, regardless of wealth?

The Purposes and Scope of Legal Aid

If legal services were regarded as just another commodity in the market, this question would not arise. Just as the rich can afford better food, clothing, cars and holidays, so they can afford better legal services. Is there anything wrong with that? Yes, there is: it goes against the ideal of equal access to justice as expressed by Chief Justice King. Access to justice often requires use of legal services; yet these are notoriously expensive, and many people cannot afford them. In this chapter we examine two developments designed to overcome or reduce this problem: legal aid, and new tribunals and courts.

One first thinks of legal aid, perhaps, in terms of the criminal courts: people should be entitled to defend themselves properly against criminal charges. In practice they need legal assistance to do this effectively, and should therefore be entitled to lawyers to advise and represent them. However, the same argument applies to civil actions: poor people who are unjustly evicted from their homes, or swindled by credit companies or who want divorce, are only demanding their legal rights, and should be able to find redress in the courts. Again, in practice this means they must have legal advice and representation, and the argument does not stop at the courts. A great deal of legal work is done outside the courts — drawing up wills and other documents, advising on legal problems of transferring property, family law matters and so on. In all areas, criminal and civil, whether the matter is large or small, and whether the poor person is initiating or defending court proceedings, or is seeking to arrange his or her affairs in a way that avoids court cases, legal rights are involved. To the extent that people are unable to ascertain or protect their rights through lack of funds for legal assistance, to that extent our system falls short of the ideal of equality before the law.

This might seem simple enough, but the scope and design of legal aid poses some very important questions. Firstly, in obtaining legal services, wealthy individuals can choose a specialist in the area concerned, and might obtain skilful advice on problems related to law. For example, a client with a tax problem might obtain advice not only about how to fill in tax returns but how to reorganize his or her business affairs. If legal aid is to match the sort of services available to wealthy people, the legal aid service should perhaps have expertise in such matters as tenancy and social security law, and should provide advice that will help poor people plan their affairs. For example, it makes sense to have a social worker as part of the legal aid office, since tenants thrown out of their homes often need help in finding new accommodation and obtaining social security as well as getting advice on tenancy law.

Secondly, it is arguable that the law is more responsive to the interests of the wealthy and powerful than it is to those of other people. Wealthy people and groups often lobby politicians when new legislation is being considered, and have the resources to take "test cases" on appeal to establish some point of law. If there is to be equal access to the law in a wider sense, legal aid should perhaps provide similar services to the collective interests of poor people. For example, it could make submissions for the reform of tenancy laws, rather than just helping individual tenants. It could seek, also, to influence the administration of the law, as the Aboriginal Legal Service has done in bringing to light discriminatory practices by the police or other public authorities.

In fact, however, legal aid in Australia has tended to be provided in ways that do not encourage these kinds of service. Most legal aid is in the form of service provided for individuals by lawyers in private practice, who are then paid from legal aid funds. It is necessary to describe the Australian experience in a little detail.

Legal Aid: the Australian Pattern

Up to the 1970s, legal aid was a matter for the States, not the Commonwealth. And the State governments largely left it to the private profession to provide it. On an individual basis, private lawyers would sometimes provide their services free or at a reduced rate to poor clients, or would accept an occasional court appointment to appear for individuals. Some would also do free legal work to advance causes they believed in, for example, lawyers associated with the Council for Civil Liberties would take cases where there appeared to be an infringement of civil liberties.

A more formal system of legal aid was established by the legal professional bodies: the first was established in South Australia in

1933, and the last in New South Wales in 1971. These schemes used the services of lawyers in private practice (not salaried employees). They obtained funds from government sources, from contributions by clients, and from the interest earned on clients' money held in trust by solicitors. However, they were by no means comprehensive: for example, the New South Wales scheme did not include any criminal work; and legal aid was not generally available for non-litigious work such as drawing up a will.

A second form of legal aid is that provided by public bodies. New South Wales was the leader in this field: it established a salaried service of Public Solicitors and Public Defenders in the 1940s. In addition, legal advice and information were provided by Chamber Magistrates in New South Wales, a service not provided in any other Australian jurisdiction. These services, however, were also less than comprehensive. In particular, they did not provide legal representation for defendants to criminal proceedings in magistrates' courts, which handle by far the majority of all criminal matters. Also, all schemes (except the Chamber Magistrates) included means tests which were so stringent that many people who could not afford legal services failed to obtain legal aid. For example, in 1974 a major study of legal aid found that the means test for the New South Wales Public Solicitor's Office excluded some people who were below the poverty line as fixed by the Henderson Commission, even though less than about 13 per cent of households in the State fell below the poverty line.

A third form of legal aid was the Australian Legal Aid Office (ALAO), created by the Federal Labor Government in 1973. The early vision of this service was radical and exciting, and much influenced by models from the United States. It was expected not only to provide much more comprehensive legal services but, by emphasizing preventive law and taking on "test cases", to help make the law more responsive to the needs and rights of poor people. But these high hopes were never fulfilled, for a variety of reasons. These included hostility from the private profession, constitutional difficulties, and most obviously, the fall of the Whitlam Government in 1975. With the election of a Liberal Country Party government, the ALAO settled back into being a modest scheme providing services of a limited kind, with a severe means test, in a few areas of law which were clearly within federal powers, especially proceedings under the *Family Law Act* 1975. By the late 1980s, the ALAO had been largely phased out, its role being taken over by the State legal aid commissions.

This did not, however, amount to a simple return to the past. If we compare legal aid in the early 1990s with legal aid prior to the 1970s, two major changes have occurred. First, it has become generally accepted that legal aid should be organised by a public authority, and not by the legal profession (although the legal profession of course remains heavily involved in the provision of services). As was stated in the report of the National Legal Aid Advisory Committee, *Legal Aid for the Australian Community* (1990), p 17, funding legal aid is "amongst the fundamental responsibilities of Federal, State and Territory governments in the administration of an effective and efficient legal system". Second, it now seems accepted that the Commonwealth should play a large part in funding and setting policy for legal aid. Both these changes are in our opinion desirable, and both derive in part from the briefly spectacular career of the Australian Legal Aid Office.

A fourth form of legal aid is constituted by independent legal centres. These emerged in the 1970s and were very closely associated with the reformist feeling of the early 1970s. The legal centres have sought to make legal aid more closely identified with the communities they serve. They use the services of lawyers and non-lawyers (for example, social workers), adopt an informal style designed to reduce the barriers between lawyers and clients, emphasize preventive and educational aspects of legal service, and are located in areas where there is greatest need for legal services. Legal centres draw on Federal, State and local government funding, and rely on volunteers as well as paid employees.

Community legal centres have established a significant and apparently permanent place in the range of legal aid services. Earlier tensions between the centres and the legal profession seem to have lessened. The centres have developed expertise in areas of special relevance to poor people, such as consumer credit, tenancy, social security and anti-discrimination law. Especially in New South Wales, new centres have been developed to carry on work in specialist areas: these include the Public Interest Advocacy Centre, the Welfare Rights Centre, the Intellectual Disability Centre, the Communications Law Centre, and a number of others. Community legal centres have been concerned not only with the rights of individuals but with improving the lot of underprivileged groups, and with the use of law as an instrument of social change. Their work has included bringing "test cases", which sometimes establish new principles, or dramatically draw to public attention deficiencies in the law. Publications on such topics, often sponsored by the legal centres and drawing on their experience, have increased, bringing previously ignored areas of law into the legal "mainstream", widening the issues dealt with in law schools and enabling new generations of lawyers to have a richer understanding of the operation of the law, especially its effect on people who have not traditionally had the opportunity to protect their interests through law. Sometimes, the centres sponsor publications aimed not at lawyers but at ordinary people. Such publications include general guides to the selected areas of the law, written in non-technical language, and in one case, a series of comics designed to inform young people of their rights, using language and artwork attractive to young people. These are considerable achievements, especially considering that community legal centres receive a very small portion of the legal aid budget: in NSW in 1991, for example, it was less than 2%.

Finally, there are types of legal aid that cater for particular categories of people. An example is a motoring organization that provides free or cheap legal aid for its members in relation to motor vehicle problems. The most important example of a service limited to a category of people, however, are the Aboriginal Legal Services. Commencing in Sydney in 1970 as a group of Aboriginal people and non-Aboriginal supporters both inside and outside the legal profession, the service grew very quickly after it had demonstrated its effectiveness and won acceptance in the Aboriginal community. When it gained substantial funding from the federal government in the early 1970s similar organizations were set up in various parts of the country. The organizations have provided Aboriginal people with legal services in a form that they can trust and is responsive to their needs. The common characteristics of the agencies are mainly two: the governing body is composed of Aboriginal people, and the work is done not only by lawyers but by Aboriginal field officers.

Aboriginal legal services, probably more than any others, are entitled to be called "community" legal services. Those on the governing body generally see themselves as representing Aboriginal people, or particular Aboriginal communities, as well as individuals. In addition to providing specific legal services, Aboriginal legal services have less tangible but perhaps even more important effects. They provide an opportunity for Aboriginal people to use the legal system to help advance their common interests, thereby providing a valuable model for other Aboriginal initiatives. In its early days the Aboriginal Legal Service concentrated on defending criminal prosecutions, but as it has grown it has extended its work to other matters, such as child custody cases, and, beyond traditional litigation, to such work as making land claims, making submissions to government bodies, and taking Aboriginal claims to the United Nations and other international bodies.

In an attempt to rationalise legal aid services, some States have established Legal Aid Commissions (the names vary) to coordinate legal aid. The Commonwealth has established the Office of Legal Aid and Family Services (OLAFS) (in the Attorney-General's Department) which is in charge of the Commonwealth's policy and funding of legal aid services, and a national advisory body, the National Legal Aid Advisory Committee.

Obtaining Legal Aid

Generally, obtaining legal aid requires the applicant to convince the legal aid body (1) that he or she is unable to afford the full cost of legal services (the "means test), (2) that the matter is of the kind that the service handles and (3) that the case has a reasonable chance of success. These tests limit legal aid very considerably. Means tests, even though they may be applied flexibly, are an important way of keeping legal aid expenditure in check, and there are many people who are not poor enough to pass the means test, but are not rich enough to be able to pay for adequate legal advice or representation.

The second test, too, excludes many matters. In criminal matters, legal representation is often not available for the smaller offences heard in magistrates' courts. In New South Wales, for example, it is not usually available in drink-driving matters, summons matters, or for defendants in domestic violence matters. In civil matters, legal aid is hardly ever available (except through the legal centres, where they exist) for work other than court cases, such as drawing up wills and advising on hire purchase or social security benefits — the kind of help wealthier people have in arranging their affairs and avoiding court cases.

The third test is no doubt necessary to discourage fanciful claims that waste public money, but it can also rule out unfamiliar types of cases, in which a person's rights may have been violated and, had the person been able to afford to take the risk of litigation by employing private lawyers, might have been vindicated by the courts.

While the details are too complex to go into here, and there are significant differences among the States, access to the legal system, whether to defend oneself or assert one's rights, remains to a considerable extent a luxury item that only some people can afford.

Apart from the specific requirements of the legal aid schemes, there are more subtle limitations of the use of legal aid. Poor people often see themselves as having very little influence over their circumstances: they are more likely than wealthy people to see an accident, or dismissal from employment, or eviction from their homes as part of life's inevitable misfortunes, rather than an infringement of their rights for which they might seek legal redress. They may simply not know that their rights have been infringed. In addition, there are psychological and social barriers that can discourage people from seeking legal services. These include fear of the cost of legal services and ignorance of legal aid, difficulties in getting to a solicitor's office in business hours, fear of lawyers, inability to assemble the factual material so that they can tell their story effectively to lawyers, lack of interpreters, and unfamiliarity with the basic features of the legal system.

On top of these problems, there are difficult questions, some of them political, about the way aid is to be administered. In some types of legal aid, the work is done by lawyers in ordinary practice who take "legal aid cases" along with other work. Most legal aid is of this kind. Other types use employed lawyers who work full time on a salaried basis, doing only legal aid work. There is a debate about which form of service is better. Some people argue that only the first type can bring to poor clients the independent help of private practitioners, whereas employed legal aid solicitors are more likely to offer a poorer service, to be loyal to their agency rather than to the clients, and to acquire a stigma that is said to be associated with government bureaucracies. Others argue that legal aid can be more efficient, economical and expert if it is centralized, and that specialist legal aid workers can take initiatives not possible for members of the private profession: an example is the work of the South Australian Legal Services Commission in running public education sessions to teach people how to handle their own divorces.

Another problem is the application to legal aid schemes of some of the traditional rules of the profession. For example, the rule that lawyers cannot advertise their services, if applied to legal aid schemes, may mean that the schemes are not known to those who need them. Fortunately, some of these rules are now being relaxed by some of the legal professional bodies.

The Limits of Legal Aid

Legal aid involves considerable government expenditure, on 1991–2 figures, in the order of $219 million a year nationally. Although this is a large amount, it is only about 5% of total expenditure on legal services. John Basten has pointed out that corporations and governments are able to increase their expenditure on legal matters, so it is doubtful how far increasing legal aid actually narrows the gap in power and influence between poor people and rich people. Another problem is that the high cost of lawyers means that the legal aid money is soon exhausted in serving the needs of the poor. The means tests are now rather severe, and there are many people not poor enough to be eligible for legal aid, but not rich enough to afford legal services: it is now common to say that to afford legal services you have to be either very rich or very poor! In the early 1990s, when governments are trying to reduce spending and legal costs continue to rise, it seems depressingly obvious that legal aid on its own will not bring our legal system very close to the ideal described by Chief Justice King. Access to the legal system, whether to defend oneself or assert one's rights, remains a luxury item available to the rich, or, paradoxically, to some of the poor.

What can be done? One approach is to think more creatively about legal aid. Instead of spending all the legal aid budget on large numbers of individual cases, part of it can be spent on work designed to solve or ease some underlying problems. This has been understood for some time, although some commentators would argue that legal aid agencies have not taken enough notice of the point. Here are some examples of legal aid being used in this more creative way:

1. Instead of only providing funds to defend large numbers of tenants against being evicted, the legal aid body funds research and law reform activities designed to enhance the rights of tenants in general, for example, by developing a standard form of lease (tenancy agreement) that is fairer to tenants.

2. Instead of merely providing funds to pay lawyers to deal with simple divorces, the legal aid body runs "do it yourself" divorce training sessions, so that people can, in uncomplicated cases, handle their own matters.

3. Instead of simply defending people against claims by creditors, the legal aid body sets up a credit advisory service to help people manage their financial affairs.

4. A legal aid body, aware that a proposed supermarket complex will harm poorer inner-city residents (whose local shops will be threatened and who do not have transport to the new supermarket), helps inner-city residents oppose the development.

5. A legal aid body lobbies the government for better social security, or for Aboriginal Land Rights, taking the view that promoting such changes will be of more benefit to their clients than focusing only on individual clients.

The arguments for such activities seem very strong. First, where the existing law or social arrangements prejudice the people in question, it often makes more sense to change these than to help individuals battle against unfair laws. Second, as mentioned earlier, this approach to legal aid in fact allows poor people to do what rich people and large corporations frequently do, namely use legal expertise to make submissions and lobby for legal changes and government decisions that are in their favour. Poor people don't only lack money, but also power to influence the forces that shape their lives, and if legal aid can give them some of this kind of power, then it would go some way towards giving them the kind of access to law that is available to the more rich and powerful. Nevertheless, governments can sometimes be reluctant to fund activities which seem to "rock the boat", or conflict with government policy; and cautious legal aid administrators are likely to prefer the more familiar and comfortable approach of providing traditional kinds of assistance to individuals who are taken to court or wish to go to court to protect their interests.

It is probably true that the examples given here remain the exception rather than the rule, and are rarely carried out, except by community legal centres and the Aboriginal Legal Services. The development of legal aid since the 1970s has undoubtedly provided many poor people with assistance, and this is a genuine achievement. But it has fallen far short of the aspirations of many who agitated for legal aid in the 1960s and 70s, seeing it as a means whereby underprivileged groups could use law as a means of social and legal reform.

Alternative Approaches: Newer Forms of Dispute Resolution

The apparent failure of legal aid to achieve the ideals of some of its enthusiastic supporters has led some people to turn elsewhere to find some measure of justice for poor people. They feel it is necessary to make use of other ways of resolving disputes, ways that are cheaper, quicker than the courts and do not require the services of lawyers. These ideas may have played a part in the creation of small claims courts and tribunals. These bodies, established in the mid-1970s everywhere except Tasmania (which held out until 1985), deal with small civil matters in a way that is much less formal than the procedures of the courts, which we considered in Chapter 10. The rules of evidence do not apply; costs are not awarded to the winner; legal representation is generally not allowed; and the magistrate (or other adjudicator) adopts a much more "inquisitorial" role than does a judge in the normal courts. There are two types of bodies. In some States, they are simply the ordinary lower courts with modified procedures, dealing with a variety of small claims. In other States, however, there are special tribunals, dealing only with claims by consumers against traders, and presided over not by magistrates but by referees, who might not even have legal training.

It is good that these bodies have become an accepted part of the Australian legal system. They do something to offset the disadvantages that consumers have in the ordinary courts: manufacturers and retailers deal with similar everyday cases, employ lawyers to advise them on presenting the case, and have funds available for appeal if they should lose, whereas consumers usually have none of these advantages. Despite their impact in consumer affairs however, small claims courts and tribunals have not made much impact on the courts generally. Perhaps they are unlikely to do so, since their focus has been with consumers as much as with court reform, and the ordinary court system is very much under the control of the legal profession, which is unlikely to encourage the extension to other areas of the processes of small claims tribunals and courts.

We should mention also the establishment of "community justice centres" in New South Wales. These are centres where people are brought together to help them resolve their disputes by agreement; they are really mediation centres. They do not produce legally binding orders (unlike the small claims bodies). They work best to solve disputes between neighbours and other people who have a continuing relationship, and where neither is more powerful than the other. Again, there is no evidence that these bodies are likely to lead to a serious challenge to the traditional courts.

Community Justice Centres are an important and influential example of the use of mediation in legal disputes. In recent years, other forms of mediation have grown up, and have acquired the general title of "alternative dispute resolution". One can find examples in areas as diverse as commercial law, environmental law and family law, and ADR includes services associated with courts as well as separate services. Enthusiasts for ADR claim that it can help people resolve their problems without recourse to costly and distressing litigation, and that use of ADR helps people keep control of their own lives, and as well as helping them resolve a particular dispute helps them learn skills in coping with other disputes in their lives. More cautious observers point out that ADR has dangers. Where there is a power imbalance between the parties, the processes and outcomes of bargaining may favour the stronger. ADR may help mask a situation where people cannot enforce their rights. Like other attempts to modify the legal system to make it more accessible to underprivileged groups, ADR can be criticised as offering second-class justice to the poor. Our view is that ADR techniques can be a real benefit if used appropriately, but that we have much to learn about designing systems that lead to the appropriate use of ADR and avoid the pitfalls that the critics have identified.

We leave the subject of legal aid and access to justice in a more sober spirit than we did in our first edition. Legal aid is now an established part of the legal system, and there are promising initiatives in modifying the legal system to make it more appropriate for the concerns of less privileged people. However the changes fall far short of what would be required to produce real equality. Perhaps this is inevitable. We suspect that even a relatively liberal system of legal aid, and well-designed modifications to the legal system, can reduce only slightly the gap between rich and poor in access to legal services, and legal rights. Economic indicators show that in recent decades the gap between rich and poor has been widening, and it is difficult to imagine a realistic program of legal aid that would significantly reduce the consequent inequality of enforceable legal rights. Despite its considerable merits, the Australian system of legal aid cannot save the community from the classic jibe that "the law is open to both rich and poor — just like the Ritz Hotel".

12
Individual Liberty and Public Power

Pressures Against Liberty

One of the central tasks — perhaps the central task — in any legal and political system is to combine order with freedom. Living in society necessarily means that people accept some limits to their freedom of action as individuals in return for the various benefits of being a member of an organized community.

Some of those limits are accepted in the interest of the freedom of other individuals. My freedom to wave my right arm around stops where your nose begins; my freedom to play my records loudly ceases where it bothers my next door neighbour. We generally leave it to parliaments and judges to define the various points where one person's freedom must yield to the interests of other people.

Other limits are accepted as necessary to allow Governments themselves to take action in the interest of society as a whole. Nowadays we require our Governments to do lots of things such as regulating the economy, maintaining order, controlling pure food standards, providing schools, licensing trades and professions, zoning land use and the like. To do these various things, for the benefit of all of us, Governments have to be given considerable powers, but the exercise of these powers may adversely affect some of us. It may be to society's benefit that a new freeway be built, but your home may have to be pulled down to make way for it. And, in order that thieves be caught, it may be necessary to give the police power to enter and search peoples' houses.

Does it follow, as societies become larger and their affairs become more complex, that Governments will inevitably be given increasing powers, that the law will increasingly limit individual freedom, and that the scope for individual liberty will decrease almost to vanishing point?

This, we suppose, can happen if the people are not particularly concerned about individual freedom and if they regard the individual's interests as always subordinate to those of society. It has happened in countries where a political party or dictator wins power and imposes a "totalitarian" form of government on the people. It may not even have to be imposed; a majority of people may be prepared to accept it if the Government is able to improve their lives in other ways such as by eliminating starvation or redistributing land.

In other words, the importance attached to individual liberty varies from country to country and, often, from one period to another. There are some countries, like Britain, the United States and Australia, which claim to have an almost unbroken tradition of respect for individual freedom. If we accept this claim, and consider it to be a good thing, it's worth trying to understand what there is in our political and legal system which allows it to happen. It's also worth considering whether, in the face of increasing government power, new arrangements may be needed to protect individual liberty against erosion.

Traditions and Institutional Arrangements

A recurring theme throughout British history has been the notion that Government should be subject to law. The idea is that law, and legal rules, make it possible for people to know in advance the extent of Governmental powers and the legal remedies available against their abuse. Such laws should also be of general application. "The rule of law" thus stands in contrast to favouritism and discrimination, and to the possibility of individual rights being at the whim and mercy of the Government.

This idea has found expression in Magna Carta, in the great British constitutional struggles of the seventeenth century and in the Constitution of the United States of America. It is, above all, a tradition and an instinct about justice, but in terms of law and Government it rests on several propositions:

1. The mere fact that a person is King, Governor, Minister, official or police officer does not, of itself, give him or her any more power to affect your rights than any private person has — any special powers will exist only if clearly given *by law*. (This legal rule, while impor-

tant, does not help in a situation where a King or Dictator — or Cabinet — can dominate Parliament or the courts and thus acquire the legal powers they may want.)

2. Probably the most significant support for "the rule of law" is found in the proposition that legislation, the formal enactment of law, is properly the function of a body which is representative of the nation. This idea dates in Britain at least from the thirteenth century when Parliament was born. Parliament is not only *representative* of the people but is also responsible to them — it has to be elected every few years, and if the people do not like what one Parliament has done they can elect different people to sit in the new Parliament.

3. A further institutional arrangement concerns the executive Government — the people who, at the highest level, direct the day-to-day running of Government (Cabinet in our system). They too, must be *responsible* to the people, directly as in the American system, or indirectly through Parliament as in the British and Australian system. This idea of responsible Government was established in Britain after many centuries of struggle.

4. British experience, especially in the seventeenth century, also showed that it was important to protect judges from any pressures from Parliament or executive. Judges are supposed to decide disputes on the basis of law — legislation or case law. If the Government can dismiss a judge at any time, then the judge may well be reluctant to decide a dispute in a way that would displease the Government. As noted in Chapter 8, judges of the higher courts are therefore usually appointed for life, or until a fixed retiring age; and usually they can be dismissed only for proven misbehaviour or incapacity, and only on the basis of a resolution of both Houses of Parliament.

It is, of course, possible for a Government to *appoint* as judges men or women who, the Government expects, will decide cases in the way the Government wishes. Such matters may tip the scales in favour of one among several suitable candidates but, fortunately, our governments have not made blatantly "political" appointments of incompetent judges. Only tradition and community values prevent this — there are in Australia no legal or institutional safeguards.

The above propositions are valuable as far as they go. In 2, 3 and 4 we referred, respectively, to the legislature, the executive and the judiciary. These are the three traditional arms of Government which, according to the theory of separation of powers, should be distinct from each other. One body (the legislature) enacts the law, another (the executive) applies the law, and the third (the judiciary) decides disputes, civil and criminal, arising from the law. This pat theory of distinct functions does not completely accord with reality. We have already seen that judges participate in making law, and a role of the courts generally is to ensure that Governmental action is kept within the law. In other respects the judiciary does stand distinct.

Where the theory really breaks down is in the relationship between the legislature and the executive which are closely linked in our system. Those who form the Cabinet do so solely because they are leading members of the political party (or coalition of parties) whose supporters have a majority in the Lower House of Parliament. According to the classical theory Parliament controls the Government. A vote against the Government on an important matter in the Lower House can lead to the fall of the Government, and the Government depends on Parliament to vote the moneys it needs to govern and to pass its laws.

As we suggested in Chapter 5, in practice it seems more correct to say today that Government controls Parliament. It is able to do so primarily because of the party system — the leaders of the Government are also leading members of the majority party and therefore have important disciplinary power over that majority. Ministers usually have more information at their disposal than "backbenchers" can have, and it is the Cabinet which arranges and runs the business of Parliament.

It seems, then, that those who are involved in running the country (or the State) can usually count on Parliament passing the laws they want, and for all their independence, judges must apply such laws.

A Government will be unlikely to *want* Parliament to pass laws which a majority of electors may consider obnoxious, if only because they may lose votes at the next elections. However, what is there in the above propositions to protect *minorities?* Nothing. Their fate depends on the prevailing sense of justice in the community and on their political power to influence voters. These factors may prevent the passage of an Act of Parliament which directly encroaches on their interests. However, a greater danger arises from statutes which give powers to the administration in very wide terms. The implications of such a power may not be realized until it is actually exercised, in an oppressive or unjust way. What remedies does the law provide?

Legal Protections and Legal Restraints

For the most part there are very few legal limitations on legislative power in our system designed to protect the individual against undue encroachments on liberty, or against arbitrary action by Government. Such protections as we do have are political — the political responsibility of Government and legislature to the electorate and, above all, a political tradition of freedom. Whether they are sufficient remains to be considered.

By contrast the United States Constitution includes "Bill of Rights" provisions specifically designed to protect the individual against the Government. This means that a citizen whose rights are infringed by Governmental actions can ask the court to rule that such actions (and even statutes) are invalid. Many other nations have adopted Bills of Rights; Britain and Australia have not.

Actually the Commonwealth Constitution does contain a few provisions which appear to protect individual rights, directly or indirectly. Thus, for example, s 116 speaks of religious freedom, and s 51 (xxxi) requires the Commonwealth (not the States) to provide fair compensation when it acquires property. Such provisions have proved to be of minor value. The major exception is the promise in s 92 of freedom of "trade, commerce and intercourse among the States", and the main impact of this is on commercial transactions.

Beyond a few such scattered provisions, there are no entrenched rules in Federal or State law to make illegal any law which authorizes interference with fundamental human rights of the citizen. How then do such rights and liberties stand?

Consider freedom of expression. This seems to suggest that I can say or write whatever I like, but even in a country which has a Bill of Rights certain limits are seen to be necessary.

One limit arises from the fact that what I want to say about you may cause other people to think badly of you. You are as much entitled to have your reputation protected from unjustified attack as I am to say what I like. Therefore my freedom of expression is limited by the laws of defamation — you can sue me for damages if I tell people something unjustified about you which harms your reputation.

Nothing said about you in Parliament or the law courts, however, will give you a right to sue. The reason is a belief, recognized by law, that in these arenas, full discussion and the search for truth should not be hampered by fear of possible legal liability. On the other hand your freedom to say what you think about Parliament, and the courts themselves, is limited by the legally recognized proposition that the authority and independence of these institutions require special protection. If you publish something which may interfere with the fair trial of a case in court or with the proper functioning of Parliament or parliamentarians, or if you publish something critical of these institutions which "goes too far" so as possibly to lower their authority in the eyes of the public, then you may be punished for contempt of court or of Parliament.

Another limitation arises from a consideration of what is taken to be the community's sense of decency. There are legal controls on books etc, which may be imported into Australia (under Commonwealth law) or which are published in Australia (under State law). There are separate censorship arrangements for films, videos, television and radio, theatre, and other forms of expression. The key word which has usually been used in this area of restriction is "obscenity", a term which is now generally applied as indicating something which does not conform with current community standards of decency. There is occasional controversy about this restriction on expression. In practice it is mainly expression on matters of sex or violence which is restricted and this raises the kind of issues considered in the next chapter.

There are other restrictions on freedom of expression. For example, it is an offence to urge people to overthrow the Government by violence, or to provoke hostility and ill-will between different classes of Her Majesty's subjects in order to threaten a breach of the peace.

These are just some of the restrictions on freedom of expression recognized by Australian law. In each case there is thought to be a good reason for the restriction — some countervailing interest of other individuals or of the community as a whole which is believed to need protection.

Even a country which does expressly confer a *right* of free expression in a Bill of Rights will recognize that such freedom cannot be absolute. Thus American law recognizes legal liability for defamation, obscenity, sedition and the like. But a guarantee will usually have the effect of requiring that any such restrictions be closely defined and that they should go no further than is absolutely necessary to protect the relevant interest, otherwise the courts may hold them to be invalid.

Australian law has been criticized at a number of points on the ground that some of the restrictions in our system are excessive. In the absence of an entrenched Bill of Rights guarantee (in the absence, in other words, of any legal restriction on permissible legal restrictions of freedom) Australians can rely only on political factors to keep such restrictions to a minimum. If they feel no great concern about these issues, then freedom of expression may become subject to greater legal restriction than is perhaps necessary.

The Australian legal system, in short, at no point gives or recognizes a positive right to free expression. The law is concerned only with the various legal restrictions on freedom. Anything which does not give rise to legal liability may, as far as the courts are concerned, be freely said or written. The only way to know what you may safely say, then, is to find out what the law says you may not say — anything else is permissible. Freedom in Australia is not so much fundamental as residual.

Human Rights — Recent Developments

This simplified picture of the Anglo-Australian tradition in regard to individual liberties needs to be qualified in the light of a number of developments over the past decade or so. Australian governments have continued to resist proposals to enact enforceable, generalized Bills of Rights, but some have established institutional arrangements to deal with particular issues.

For example, New South Wales has a Privacy Committee with power to investigate complaints of violations of privacy and to attempt to resolve them; and an Anti-Discrimination Board to attempt to resolve complaints about discrimination on grounds of race, sex and certain other grounds, coupled with last-resort powers of enforcement through an Equal Opportunity Tribunal. Victoria, South Australia, Western Australia, Queensland and the ACT also have anti-discrimination and equal opportunity machinery.

At the Federal level, there is a Human Rights and Equal Opportunity Commission. The Commission consists of a President, a Human Rights Commissioner, a Race Discrimination Commissioner, a Privacy Commissioner and a Sex Discrimination Commissioner. The last three Commissioners have particular responsibility for complaints under the *Racial Discrimination Act* 1975 (Cth), the *Sex Discrimination Act* 1984 (Cth) and the *Privacy Act* 1988 (Cth). The processes under these Acts require attempts to conciliate before court proceedings may be instituted. The Commission also has more general powers of conciliation, education, and so on, in regard to alleged violations of the rights listed in the *International Covenant on Civil and Political Rights* and several other international instruments.

Australia has ratified a number of international human rights treaties in regard to such matters as racial discrimination, discrimination against women, civil and political rights, economic social and cultural rights. The Government is obliged to provide periodic reports to international agencies as to Australian compliance with these treaties. Through legislation and other means, it is becoming possible for Australians to assert such internationally recognized rights within Australia. In addition, in 1991 Australia formally ratified the *First Optional Protocol to the International Covenant on Civil and Political Rights* so that Australians may now communicate directly to the Human Rights Committee established under the

Convention for any violation of Covenant obligations, provided that remedies within Australia are not available.

Administrative Power

In discussing the "classic" civil liberties such as personal freedom, freedom of expression, freedom of worship and the like, we are dealing with a situation where Government itself may be relatively inactive. The law (legislation or judge-made law) simply marks boundaries, so to speak, beyond which the individual's freedom ceases and legal liability commences.

Today, however, the individual's freedom of action is more likely to be limited by Government activity. We are, to borrow a phrase, "a much-governed nation". There is little we do that is not governed in some way by some Department, Board, Authority or Council.

Consider a day in the life of Jane Citizen, a resident of Sydney. She wakes from a deep dream of peace and turns on her radio to check the time. Power for the radio is supplied by courtesy of Sydney Electricity and the Electricity Commission of NSW, for which she has to pay quarterly bills. She may tune in to a commercial station, broadcasting under a licence issued on the recommendation of the Australian Broadcasting Tribunal and subject to the Tribunal's supervision and regulation. Alternatively she may prefer the programmes broadcast by another Commonwealth authority, the Australian Broadcasting Corporation. Finally she hears the time signal, provided with the aid of the Bureau of Meteorology.

After she showers with water supplied by the Water Board, she makes toast made from bread which complies with standards laid down by the State Department of Public Health. Administrative decisions will also determine whether the milk for her tea comes from New South Wales or Victoria.

Then Jane Citizen goes to work. She may travel on a bus or train run by the Urban Transit Authority or perhaps drive to work on roads made and maintained by other public bodies, provided that her car is registered and covered by compulsory third-party insurance, and that she has a driver's licence issued by the Roads and Traffic Authority. And so the day goes on.

None of this is particularly controversial, and, normally, none of it will cause any problem. It simply serves to illustrate the extent to which modern Government is involved in the details of everyday life. The pattern is similar in other modern countries.

Generally most Australians expect Government to provide services, and will complain if it does not seem to be doing enough.

However, if Jane Citizen wants Government to do things, or if the Government chooses to do things, the result will be *lots* of Government — departments, boards, officials, etc, and Government will need lots of power. Inevitably, exercise of that power will affect individual rights, as noted on p 122. Even in an age when, in many countries, the role of government is being reduced, many basic functions will continue to be performed by governments.

Governmental power takes various forms. *Administrators* may make law, for example, in the form of regulations, ordinances, bylaws and the like as we saw in Chapter 5. *Administrative tribunals* outside the court system can decide a wide variety of matters affecting your rights, for example, discipline in the public service, wage levels, tariff rates, workers' compensation, appeals against land valuation, and much more (see Chapter 9). *Public servants* can run power lines across your garden, zone your house as a home unit area, refuse you a pension, and impound your dog.

All this raises the issue discussed above: what is to prevent power of this sort from being arbitrary or tyrannical? What restrictions, what controls are there on the exercise of Governmental power?

Parliamentary Control

If Parliament by statute grants excessive power to the administration then, in theory, the electors can vote for the Opposition party next time. In practice the matter is highly unlikely to constitute any sort of clear-cut election issue, and Australian Parliaments have been content to pass statutes conferring very broad powers on administrative bodies, whatever political party is in office. This political protection is therefore of minimal value in practice.

One recent innovation, a Scrutiny of Bills Committee in the federal Senate, plays a useful watchdog role in alerting parliamentarians about bills which appear to confer excessive powers.

But even if Parliament tends to grant broad powers in the first place, it retains power to supervise what use is made of such powers.

Parliament has evolved procedures for oversight of delegated legislation as noted in Chapter 5. When it comes to Parliamentary review of individual grievances, it is common practice for citizens to approach their local member of Parliament to see if they will take up the matter with the Department or body concerned, or with the Minister. Much of a Member of Parliament's time is spent trying to do something about Mrs Jones' pension or Mr Smith's telephone bill.

If the MP receives no satisfaction from the Department he or she can, in the last resort, ask a question in Parliament, directed to the appropriate Minister. This will (perhaps) attract the attention of Parliament and even the public to the grievance and may be effective in getting redress. The administration as a whole is responsible, through Ministers, to Parliament, and if a serious fault in the administration is brought to light, the Minister is (in theory) answerable and may, in the last resort, be forced to resign.

Parliamentary review along these lines, though, is seldom very effective. Some members will be good at handling grievances for their constituents, but others may not be, and those of the Government party will often not want to embarrass their own party and its leaders by asking a question in the House. Because private members have no access to departmental files, they may have no means of knowing whether the Minister's reply to their question is satisfactory or not. Even if a Minister's "head" does "roll" (and it seldom does in Australia unless the Minister was personally at fault), this may not lead to any redress of the individual grievance which started the whole thing. At best, Parliamentary review is a hit-and-miss affair.

Ombudsmen

In recent times there has been growing enthusiasm for the idea of the Ombudsman. An Ombudsman is neither a mythical beast nor a Nordic gnome, but an officer appointed specifically to investigate complaints by people as to the way in which they have been treated by the administration.

The office originated in Scandinavia. In the past three decades the idea spread to many other parts of the world including New Zealand, Britain, Canada, the United States and, now, all Australian jurisdictions. There are differences in detail in the powers and procedures of individual Ombudsmen, but the following summary gives a general picture.

A person may lodge a complaint with the Ombudsman who will then discuss it with the Department or public authority concerned. More often than not, any unfairness or injustice will be remedied there and then; or the Ombudsman may be able to give the complainant a satisfactory explanation for the action complained of. But the Ombudsman can proceed to investigate by interviewing officials and examining files, and will eventually make a report and recommendations. If the report is against the Department or agency, and they fail to accept the Ombudsman's recommendations, he or she can report to Parliament. The Ombudsman cannot override decisions, but can be very persuasive. As well as resolving individual grievances, the Ombudsman can recommend changes in procedures and in the law itself in order to prevent such grievances arising in the first place.

Judicial Control

However, there are also some legal limitations on Government action. That is, there are certain grounds upon which administrative action can be challenged in the courts, and if the challenge is successful the action will be prevented or reversed. The principle is that Governmental power must be exercised according to law, and if it is not the courts can rule it invalid.

Broadly speaking, the courts use the following principles. Firstly, where there is statutory power for an administrative agency to do something, the agency may use that power to do only what is authorized. Thus, if a statute gives a Minister power to make regulations governing the sale of fireworks, and he or she makes regulations governing the sale of soap, those regulations will be *ultra vires* (that is, beyond power) and invalid. If a tribunal has power to fix wages for employees in the catering industry, and it makes an award covering night club dancers, this award may be held invalid.

Even if the action taken is what is authorized, a court may hold this action invalid if it has been done improperly in some way, for example, if it was done for a purpose other than that for which the power was given; or if it was done on the basis of irrelevant considerations; or if it was so unreasonable that no reasonable agency would have exercised the power in that way; or if the agency has clearly misunderstood its powers; or if it has simply applied an inflexible policy rule; or if it has really left the decision to someone else.

In addition, action may also be held *ultra vires* if essential procedures prescribed by legislation have not been complied with. The courts, too, will in some cases prescribe procedural requirements of their own by saying that certain types of power which may affect you (for example, to demolish your house or expel you from a union) may only be validly exercised if you are first given a fair hearing. If you are not allowed an adequate chance to present your case, or if the hearing you are given is in some way unfair, then the court may invalidate what has been done on the ground that there has been a denial of "natural justice" or "procedural fairness".

The courts have the power to review administrative action along these lines even when there is no formal right of appeal, and even where power has been conferred in very wide terms. They can do so through a variety of procedures bearing mysterious names such as certiorari, prohibition, mandamus, actions for a declaration, injunction and others. Some of these procedures are as antique and complex as their names suggest. There has also been much technicality about the grounds on which the remedies may be granted.

However, in the past 30 years there has been considerable liberalization of the law on judicial review. Some of this has been achieved by the judges in taking a much more activist role in overseeing administrative action in a series of major cases. But Parliaments have also intervened to simplify review procedures in some jurisdictions (for example, Commonwealth, Victoria) and to make judicial review easier in other ways (for instance, by requiring decision-makers to give reasons). Freedom of Information Acts in several jurisdictions also allow general access to documents held by government, subject to exemptions.

Nonetheless judicial review is properly concerned only with the *legality* of the action under challenge, not with the *facts* or the *merits*. A very different judicial procedure is appeal which will normally allow oversight of every aspect of a decision appealed against (that is, facts, law and merits), but there is no right to appeal against a decision unless statute creates such a right. Statutes sometimes do and sometimes do not give a right to appeal against decisions by Departments and public authorities. And rights of appeal, when given, may be appeal to another administrator or the Minister, or to a tribunal, or to an inferior court, an intermediate court, or a superior court. It may be a full right of appeal, or limited to questions of law.

One of the most important innovations in the Commonwealth Parliament's "new administrative law" is the *Administrative Appeals Tribunal Act* 1975. This Act established the Administrative Appeals Tribunal (AAT), made up of judges, lawyers and non-lawyers, to hear appeals from a wide range of decisions made by administrators and tribunals under federal statutes, and its jurisdiction has been steadily expanded over the years. From the AAT's decisions there is a further right of appeal (on points of law only) to the Federal Court of Australia.

The same Act also established a high-level Administrative Review Council to keep continual oversight over the workings of the AAT, the Commonwealth Ombudsman, the *Administrative Decisions (Judicial Review) Act* 1977 (which gives the Federal Court judicial review powers under simplified procedures), and the general question of review of federal administrative action.

While all States have established Ombudsmen, and some have simplified judicial review procedures, none except Victoria have gone as far as the Commonwealth in its attempts to develop a coherent system of administrative law.

We have hundreds of tribunals. We have over a million Government employees working for departments, statutory authorities, commissions, boards, local councils etc. Many of these people have been given, by statute, extensive powers to make regulations or to decide how we are to be treated in one way or another. Even if they exercise these powers with care and in good faith, injustices do occur and all too often there is no redress.

Australians expect a great deal from their Governments. Governments, at all levels, must have powers, and the exercise of those powers will inevitably affect individual rights from time to time. But if "the rule of law" is to be maintained, interference with individual rights should be kept to a minimum. It should be subject to procedures designed to establish fairness and impartiality, and it should, in appropriate cases, be subject to review — review within the administration itself, or review by Parliament, or review by an Ombudsman, or review in the courts.

The Australian legal and governmental systems are not yet fully adequate to deal with these problems of modern government, and too little attention has been given to the question of how to maintain a proper relationship between governmental power on the one hand and individual rights on the other.

Big Government is no doubt here to stay, even if there are fluctuations in the role assigned to it. But if "rule of law" ideals are to be maintained and civil liberties protected, it must also be fair Government, providing the fullest safeguards for individual rights and freedoms.

This is one of the principal problem areas in the Australian legal system, and only in the last three decades has it begun to receive the attention it deserves, particularly at Commonwealth level.

13

Law and Morality

There is a characteristic moral tone about law. The law is full of words like "fair", and "proper", and "dishonest". In courts, there is often as much talk of "propriety" as legality; of "fault" as of liability; of "wickedness" as of criminality. For many non-lawyers (and probably a few lawyers) law is closely bound up with morality, and it is assumed that somehow the law must be "right", and that everyone has a duty to comply with it.

The vague but persistent connection between law and morality has been of great interest to legal philosophers, and much has been written about it, but it's not merely of interest to egg-heads. Consider people wondering whether to cheat on their tax return; or a doctor, wondering whether to switch off the life-support apparatus for a terminally ill patient; or a minister of a government committed to an anti-uranium policy, deciding whether to honour uranium contracts made by the previous government. What these people think (or assume without thinking) about the relationship between law and morality is very likely to affect the decisions they make.

The subject is large and controversial, but it seems to involve at least four separate questions:

- Can an immoral law still be a "law"?
- Is there a duty to obey the law?
- Does the law reflect a society's morality?

- Should the criminal law be used to enforce morality by punishing acts because they are considered immoral?

Let us take these in turn.

Can an Immoral Law still be a Law?

Law is clearly distinct from morality. The law on abortion, for example, can be changed with a stroke of the legislative pen, while changes of public opinion on moral questions are slower and less obvious. There are many opinions about the morality of abortion in each Australian State, but each State has only one law on abortion: therefore the law could not be the same as everyone's moral views. It need not necessarily reflect the majority opinion (if there is one). Law is one thing, morality another. A particular law may or may not reflect the moral views held by you, or us, or the majority of people in the community.

All this seems obvious, yet some legal philosophers have argued, sometimes quite passionately, that laws which are very immoral, and violate fundamental human rights, do not deserve to be called "law" at all. The racist laws of Nazi Germany in the past, and of South Africa today, are sometimes given as examples of "laws" which are so fundamentally unjust that they should not be called laws at all. The argument is often made in connection with the question of obedience to law, for some people think that if such rules are not regarded as "law" then there is no duty to obey them.

We do not find this analysis very helpful. In Chapter 1 we identified law as those rules which will be recognized and enforced in the courts. Some laws, such as those which tell you how to make a will, seem morally neutral; other laws, such as those prohibiting fraud, may seem perfectly acceptable; others, such as laws prohibiting homosexual acts between adult males in private, we may think are immoral. But it does not seem helpful to say that the laws we do not like are not laws at all. Calling these provisions "law" does not imply that we approve of them or think that they should necessarily be obeyed, or even respected. It seems clearer to say that they are laws, but unjust laws which should be repealed, and perhaps, should not be obeyed — which brings us to the next question.

Is There a Duty to Obey the Law?

This is an important question for people faced with laws to which they deeply object. For example, it faces the pacifist conscript, and the doctor who is asked to perform an illegal abortion, or to assist a terminally ill patient who wishes to die. It also faces people who have been refused permission to hold a demonstration for which permission is required, and soldiers ordered to kill civilians in a war. They have to decide whether to obey the law or their conscience. Such choices can be agonizing, and no amount of legal or philosophical analysis will make them easy, although it may clarify the nature of the choice to be made. It is important to realize that the question "is there a duty to obey the law?" is ambiguous. For "duty" could refer to a legal duty or a moral duty. If it refers to a *legal* duty, the answer is yes, by definition: the pacifist conscientious objector, the abortionist and the mercy-killer are all breaking the law, and may go to gaol, but they know this only too well. The real question is, whether there is a *moral* duty to obey the law.

This is a question of personal morality, not a question of law, and there is no particular reason why a lawyer should know the answer. Some people argue that there is a moral duty to obey the law, whatever it is, while it is the law; all you can do is try to have it changed. For us, this answer is too dogmatic. We can see the argument that society functions better if people generally keep the law — though this assumes that the present form of society is worth preserving — but we would not be prepared to give up the (moral) right to disobey a law if we thought we should. You, of course, will have to make up your own mind.

Does the Law Reflect Society's Morality?

The third question is a factual, sociological question: does the law reflect a society's morality? While we are no sociologists, we have no doubt the answer is yes. The criminal law, in particular, seems in its broad outlines to be much influenced by the community's views about what is immoral. There is nothing approaching complete coincidence of moral rules and legal rules, of course. Thus many forms of vindictiveness and greed may be widely condemned as immoral but may nevertheless be perfectly legal, and many crimes, particularly involving motor cars, would not generally be thought to be immoral. A further qualification is that there is not a single moral view held by "the community". People have different views, and those views may vary according to many factors, ranging from individual differences to attitudes held by particular groups of people, defined by a range of matters including gender, race, income and social class, education, and many others. This important qualification should not however be overstated: in our view it is correct to say that on many fundamental issues the criminal law reflects views that are very widely held in the community.

There is a related question: does the law itself influence a society's moral views? This is much more difficult to answer, but it seems likely that the law is one of the factors that influences current moral views, particularly as many people think it "right" to comply with the law. For example, it might be that relaxing laws on pornography contributes to a more liberal attitude on matters of sexual expression in the community generally. Again, removing laws that criminalise homosexual practices between consenting adult males may contribute to reducing the extent to which people think of such practices as immoral. Some legal systems go further than ours in attempting to use the law as a form of community education. A Swedish law, for example, forbids parents to use corporal punishment on their children. It seems likely that the Swedish lawmakers knew perfectly well that this law would hardly ever be enforced, but felt that it would contribute to a climate in which corporal punishment would be seen as unacceptable. You might be able to think of some Australian laws that also seem to have a "educative" purpose.

Should the Criminal Law be Used to Enforce Morality?

We now come to a most difficult, interesting and controversial question: how far, if at all, should society enforce community morality through the criminal law? Should certain types of conduct be criminal because they are generally regarded as immoral by community standards?

Although the issue relates to morality in general, the debate has often focused on sexual morality. There seem to be two reasons for this. The first is the curious way morality is often taken to *mean* sexual morality. Thus, when we speak of a person on a "morals" charge we mean a charge of some kind of sexual misconduct; murderers, thieves and drunken drivers are not said to be on "morals" charges. A second reason why this debate centres on sexual offences is that it is in this area that the question is most clearly raised. Most other crimes are punished not merely because they are immoral but also for other reasons. We convict and punish murderers and thieves because we want to protect our lives and property: we do not do it merely because we see their conduct as immoral, although no doubt that comes into it. In sexual offences, however, sometimes it often seems that we are punishing *immorality as such*.

Some of these crimes are often said to be crimes without victims. Male homosexual practices, for instance, between consenting adults in private, are still a criminal offence in some Australian States. These laws, of course, existed long before anyone had heard of the Acquired Immune Deficiency Syndrome (AIDS). This fatal and presently incurable disease can be sexually transmitted, and in western countries appears to have been spread mainly through homosexual activities and sharing of needles by intravenous drug users. The question whether the law should be used in the fight against AIDS, and if so, how, is a difficult one. It is surely wrong, however, to say that the problem of AIDS justifies laws criminalising homosexual practices. It is quite fanciful to think that such a law would in fact stop sexual activity between homosexuals. Further, it would undermine the very valuable work done by the gay community, in co-operation with medical experts, to promote the use of "safe sex" practices. AIDS nevertheless illustrates an important point about our argument. "Private" activities sometimes have the potential to affect the community; think of a maniac, quietly working at home developing deadly bacteria capable of poisoning a large city. To the extent that they do, the argument about law shifts from the punishment of immorality as such to the protection of the community against harm. This is clearly a proper function of the law, but our present concern is whether the law can legitimately be used to prohibit behaviour on the ground of its "immorality", as distinct from its possible harmful effects.

There are many other examples of types of conduct which seem to be criminal only, or mainly, because they are immoral. Many forms of common sexual conduct are criminal even between married people. Of course, many of these offences are not enforced in practice, and such studies as the Kinsey Report suggest that a large proportion of the population owe their present freedom to this fact. Other areas which raise the issue include prostitution, pornography, frank language and abortion. There are also relevant areas outside sexual morality; for example, the use of certain drugs, or certain forms of gambling. Attempted suicide, too, is an offence in some States, as is euthanasia, even in cases of extreme distress and with the consent of the victim. In all these areas, the fact that the conduct is generally regarded as "immoral" seems the central reason why it is illegal. It may not be the only reason; for example, the laws against incest may be motivated also by considerations of eugenics, and soliciting for prostitution may be also concerned with protecting the public's sensibilities. But it is clear that in such areas the law largely reflects the notion that the fact that conduct is immoral is good reason for making it criminal.

There are two extreme positions in this debate. The philosopher John Stuart Mill said:

> The only purpose for which power can rightfully be exercised over any member of a civilized community against his will is to prevent harm to others.

At the other extreme is a famous Victorian judge, James Stephen:

> Criminal law in this country actually is applied to the suppression of vice and so to the promotion of virtue to a very considerable extent: and this I say is right.

In more recent times the debate has been carried on in England by Lord Devlin and Professor H L A Hart, whose books are noted in the reading guide.

We are very much in agreement with Mill and Hart on this matter. We do not think that it is legitimate to use the criminal law to punish immorality as such. For example, we think that laws making criminal private homosexual acts between consenting adult males should be repealed; such laws have been repealed in some places, and society, as far as we know, appears to have survived the experience.

Here are our reasons:

1. The effect of making acts criminal is to render those who commit them liable to punishment. Punishment involves, in this case, the deliberate infliction of suffering on people by the State. The suffering inflicted by criminal laws should not be underestimated. Who could measure, for instance, the suffering of homosexuals under the shadow of the criminal law? Apart from those who suffer the disgrace and distress of trial and punishment, consider all those who must live in the constant knowledge that their most loving relationships carry with them the threat of prosecution. Clearly, those who say that certain acts should be made crimes must show that the pain of punishment can be justified.

2. For most crimes the justification is the prevention of *harm* to people. In particular, the State has a legitimate role in seeking to protect its citizens' physical well-being against unjustified threats — so we have offences like murder, assault, rape, and so on. There are also some special cases where the State may legitimately protect people against harm that they do not understand: for example, it seems right to make it an offence for adults to have sexual relations with young children, even if the children do not protest or resist.

3. Some types of behaviour, however, are crimes even though they do not harm anybody. What justification can be offered for making such acts criminal?

Stephen's view, quoted above, is that the business of the criminal law is the suppression of vice and the promotion of virtue. They are not the same thing, though. If people stop doing something to avoid going to gaol, they are probably being prudent rather than virtuous, like the shopkeeper who gives correct change because it is good for business. And who is to say what is "vice"? On homosexuality and many other things, people have different views about what is right and wrong. How can you justify using the criminal law to impose the beliefs of some people on other people?

Lord Devlin argued that it is possible to justify criminal laws that enforce the prevailing moral views of a society. He wrote that "A recognized morality is as necessary to society's existence as a recognized government" and therefore "the suppression of vice is as much the law's business as the suppression of subversive activities".

The main problem with this argument is that Lord Devlin offered no evidence that society's existence is threatened by immorality, and there does not seem to be any. It may well be that more people will do something if it is lawful (though this is not necessarily true). There seems no reason to think that this will destroy a society, though it may tend to promote a change in the society's views about whether the behaviour is right or wrong. Lord Devlin's argument implies that we should use the criminal law to help a society preserve its current moral standards, *whatever their merits*, but such laws would inhibit moral change for the better, as well as for the worse. We know that societies differ widely in their moral beliefs and practices, and that changes occur over time. In a world where problems such as starvation, the oppression of indigenous peoples, and environmental destruction might suggest that moral standards could be usefully re-examined, there seems little merit in an undiscriminating effort to preserve the moral status quo.

4. Criminal laws enforcing morality as such are not only without rational justification; they are positively harmful. Consider the following:

(a) Laws enforcing morality are notoriously ineffective. People smoke marihuana, perform abortions and engage in unorthodox sexual practices whether or not they are against the law, just as Americans drank alcohol during prohibition.

(b) Such laws often have bad side effects. The illegality of marihuana means that it is widely sold through dealers in hard drugs, and involves its users with real criminals. Illegal abortions are expensive and become the prerogative of the rich: for the poor it may be a question of unwanted children or dangerous and degrading "backyard abortions". Laws against homosexuality encourage police corruption and blackmail. You can extend the list for yourself.

(c) Enforcing laws against immorality wastes community resources. If we got rid of some of these laws we could give the police, the courts and the prisons more opportunity to reduce the millions of dollars lost in tax frauds every year, or to make city streets safe to walk in at night.

(d) These laws tend to be vague. The definition of obscenity in censorship laws, for example, frequently includes such words

> as "deprave" or "corrupt", which of course mean very different things to different people. Another example is *Shaw's* case, mentioned in Chapter 4, which created the offence of "conspiring to corrupt public morals". Any laws based on these concepts must be vague and uncertain in a society which is deeply divided about moral questions, particularly in sexual areas. Uncertainty is a dangerous thing in the law, especially the criminal law. People should be able to know what they are permitted to do and what they are not; vague laws prevent this, and make people liable to criminal penalties for carrying on what they may reasonably regard as innocent activities.

Perhaps many such laws can be justified on grounds other than the immorality of the conduct penalized. For example, one can argue that laws relating to drugs are designed to reduce a health hazard, that laws against incest are designed to reduce the number of deformed or defective children, and so on. We cannot discuss here the various considerations relating to different areas of the law, but we do say that in so far as they are designed merely to enforce morality, they are unjustifiable and should be removed. If they are to remain, they must be justified on other grounds.

The above arguments assume that it is useful to discuss the merits and demerits of these areas of law: if there are no good reasons to have such criminal penalties, then presumably they will be abolished. But it may be that this assumption (which is implicit in the very extensive published debates on this topic) is not entirely justified. It may be that the sources of these criminal laws lie more in unexamined emotions than a reasoned position. Perhaps, for example, we have a basic need for emotional reassurance and conformity which leads us to suppress groups whose life styles differ from those of "normal" members of society. Perhaps we have a need for scapegoats, and attempt to cope with aggressive or homosexual tendencies in ourselves by stamping them out in others.

To the extent that this is true, a complete account of the issue of morality and criminal law would take us beyond the sort of debates we have sketched and into an examination of the nature of people, and society, and our particular community. Such an examination, of course, would require the participation of experts in such fields as psychology, sociology, and anthropology. The topic of law and morality, therefore, illustrates an important general point about law, namely that it is a mistake to see law as a completely separate and self-contained system. On the contrary, it interacts in a complex way with the community, and a full understanding requires a study of the community, and many other things, as well as the law. This is the main reason why this book can only be an introduction, a starter. Of course, a thorough understanding of law requires the study of much legal detail. More important, it requires that the law be seen in context, and indeed many contexts. The study of law is not the study of a bundle of technical rules and procedures, but an aspect of wider study of the nature of ourselves and our society. As explained in the Introduction, we have not attempted to embark on such a study in this book, but have chosen to retain our more modest task of providing a brief introduction to law. We hope that in our efforts to "keep it simple" we have not conveyed an unduly narrow view of the law. We hope that we might have stirred the curiosity of the reader to explore the law further, and in *Additional Reading* we have set out books that should provide a good start, both for the "contextual" study of law and for those who wish to learn more about particular areas.

Additional Reading

1 INTRODUCTORY AND GENERAL TEXTS

Bartley R, *The Court is Open*, 3rd ed, Petty Publishing and Marianne Publishing, 1987.

Bates N, *Introduction to Legal Studies*, 4th ed, Butterworths, 1984.

Bird G, *The Process of Law in Australia: Intercultural Perspectives*, Butterworths, 1988.

Bowen J, *The Macquarie Easy Guide to Australian Law*, Macquarie Library, 1987.

Braybrooke E, Sinclair D and Sonnemann J, *Ignorance of the Law is No Excuse*, 2nd ed, Cheshire, 1988.

Carvan J, *Understanding the Legal System: A Book for First Time Law Students*, Montfort Press, 1991.

Castles A, *An Australian Legal History*, Law Book Co, 1982.

Council for Civil Liberties, *If You are Arrested*, 5th ed, Redfern Legal Centre Publishing, 1986.

Crawford J, *Australian Courts of Law*, 2nd ed, Oxford University Press, 1988.

De Leeuw A (ed), *Legal Resources Book* (WA). WAIT Printing Services for the Sussex Street Community Law Service, 1985.

ADDITIONAL READING

Derham D, Maher F and Waller L, *An Introduction to Law*, 6th ed, Law Book Co, 1991.

Duncan R and Roberts D (eds), *Legal Studies for New South Wales*, 2nd ed, Butterworths, 1992.

Easton D, Griffiths L, Heilbron G, Kovacs D, Latimer P and Pagone T, *Introducing the Law*, 2nd ed, CCH, 1985.

Enright C, *Studying Law*, 4th ed, Branxton Press, 1991.

Evans, M J and others, *Legal Studies for Queensland Year 12*, Butterworths, 1989.

Faine J and Nettheim G, *Pocket Guide to the Law*, Victoria, 2nd ed, Bay Books and Law Foundation of NSW, 1989.

Fitzroy Legal Service, *The Law Handbook* (Vic), 1992.

Gifford D and Gifford K, *How to Understand an Act of Parliament*, 7th ed, Law Book Co, 1991.

Gifford K and Gifford D, *Our Legal System*, 2nd ed, Law Book Co, 1983.

Graycar R and Shiff, D (eds), *Life Without Marriage: A Woman's Guide to the Law*, Pluto Press, 1987.

Healey D, White M and Nettheim G, *Pocket Guide to the Law*, New South Wales, 2nd ed, Bay Books and Law Foundation of NSW, 1988.

Krever R, *Mastering Law Studies and Exam Techniques*, Butterworths, 2nd ed, 1989.

La Legge e il Cittadino, Guida Practica alle legge de New South Wales, Ital-UIL Australia, 1990.

McKelvey C and Nunan N (eds). *Legal Resources Book (Qld)*, Caxton St Legal Service, 1983.

Morris G and others, *Laying Down the Law*, 3rd ed, Butterworths, 1992.

Pearce D and Geddes R, *Statutory Interpretation in Australia*, 3rd ed, Butterworths, 1988.

Rath P, *Our Laws — How they are Made and Maintained*, CCH, 1985.

Redfern Legal Centre, *The Law Handbook (NSW)*, 3rd ed, Redfern Legal Centre, 1988.

The Law Handbook: A New Complete Guide to the Law in South Australia, Legal Services Commission, SA, 1988.

Weeramantry, CJ, *An Invitation to the Law* Butterworths 1982.

2 ON GOVERNMENT AND PUBLIC LAW

Coper M, *Encounters with the Australian Constitution*, CCH, 1987.

Cranston, R, Law, *Government and Public Policy*, OUP 1987.

Encel S, Horne D, and Thompson E, *Change the Rules: Towards a Democratic Constitution*, Penguin, 1978.

Hanks P, *Constitutional Law in Australia*, Butterworths, 1991.

Gaze, B and Jones, M, *Law Liberty and Australian Democracy*, Law Book Co 1990.

Sawer G, *Australian Government Today*, Melbourne University Press, 13th ed, 1987.

Sawer G, *The Australian Constitution*, 2nd ed, AGPS, 1988.

Zines, L, *The High Court and the Constitution*, Butterworths, 3rd ed, 1991.

3 ON ABORIGINAL PEOPLE AND THE LAW

Hanks P and Keon-Cohen B (eds), *Aborigines and the Law*, Allen & Unwin, 1984.

Hazelhurst K (ed), *Ivory Scales: Black Australians and the Law*, New South Wales University Press, 1987.

McRae H, Nettheim, G, and Beacroft, L, *Aboriginal Legal Issues: Commentary and Materials*, Law Book Co, 1991.

Reynolds H, *Frontier*, Allen & Unwin, 1987.

Reynolds H, *The Law of the Land*, Penguin, 1987.

Reynolds H, *The Other Side of the Frontier*, Penguin, 1982.

The Law Reform Commission (Australia), *Report No 31, The Recognition of Aboriginal Customary Law*, 1986.

4 ON LEGAL AND SOCIAL THEORY RELATING TO LAW

Bottomly, S, Gunningham N, and Parker, S, *Law in Context*, Federation Press, 1991.

Devlin P, *The Enforcement of Morals*, Oxford University Press, 1968.

Dworkin R, *Law's Empire*, Fontana, 1986.

Graycar, R and Morgan J, *The Hidden Gender of Law*, Federation Press, 1990.

Hart H, *Law, Liberty and Morality*. Oxford University Press, 1963
Hart H, *The Concept of Law*, Oxford University Press, 1963.

N Naffine, *Law and the Sexes*, Allen & Unwin 1990.

O'Malley P, *Law, Capitalism and Democracy*. Allen & Unwin, 1983.

Scutt, J, *Women and the Law: Commentary and Materials*, Law Book Co, 1990.

Smart, C, *Feminism and the Power of Law*, Routledge, 1990.

Twining, W (ed) *Legal Theory and Common Law*, Blackwell 1986.

5 ON LAWYERS, LEGAL SERVICES AND THE LEGAL PROFESSION

Basten J, "Legal Aid and Community Legal Centres", (1987) 61 *ALJ* 714–724.

Astor, H and Chinkin, C, *Dispute Resolution in Australia*, Butterworths, 1992.

National Legal Aid Advisory Committee, *Legal Aid for the Australian Community*, AGPS 1990.

Disney J, Redmond P, Basten J and Ross S, *Lawyers*, Law Book Co, 2nd ed, 1986.

Fricke G, *Judges of the High Court*, Hutchinson, 1986.

Galligan B, *Politics of the High Court*, University of Queensland Press, 1987.

Kirby M, *The Judges*, Australian Broadcasting Corporation, 1983.

Ross S, *The Politics of Law Reform*, Penguin, 1982.

Sexton M, *The Legal Mystique: the Role of Lawyers in Australian Society*. Angus & Robertson, 1982.

Thomson R, *The Judges*, Allen & Unwin, 1986.

Weisbrot, D, *Australian Lawyers*, Longman Cheshire, 1990.

6 MISCELLANEOUS

Henry Cecil, A P Herbert, and more recently John Mortimer (author of the "Rumpole" series) have written humorous books about law.

Index

Authors of books referred to in the text are listed in the Index, but book titles appear in the table of Additional Reading.

Cases and statutes mentioned in the text are also included in the Index.

INDEX

Related Titles

Bates & Bates, *Legal Studies for Victoria* — Vol 1, 1990

Bates & Bates, *Legal Studies for Victoria* — Vol 2, 1991

Bird, *The Process of Law in Australia: Intercultural Perspectives*, 1988

Brown, *Western Australian Introduction to Law*, 3rd ed, 1989

Chalmers & Clark, *Legal Studies For Tasmania*, 3rd ed, 1992

Duncan & Roberts, *Legal Studies for New South Wales*, 2nd ed, 1992

Evans, Woodgate & Murphy, *Legal Studies for Queensland*, Vol 1, 2nd ed, 1992

Evans, O'Sullivan, Woodgate, Gasteen & Stewart, *Legal Studies for Queensland — Year 12*, 1989

Macadam & Smith, *Statutes*, 2nd ed, 1989

Morris, Cook, Creyke & Geddes, *Laying Down the Law*, 3rd ed, 1992

Nicholls, Gervasi, Reid & Brown (eds), *Legal Studies for South Australia, Years 11 and 12*, revised, 1991

Wells, *Law, Judges and Justice*, 1991

Notes